FIND YOUR
TRUE
NORTH

FIND YOUR
TRUE
NORTH

KANE HANSEN

First published in 2024 by Dean Publishing
PO Box 119
Mt. Macedon, Victoria, 3441
Australia
deanpublishing.com

DEAN PUBLISHING

Cataloguing-in-Publication Data
National Library of Australia
Title: Find Your True North: A True Story Of Struggle That Will Guide You To Plan
And Create Your Dream Life — No Matter Who You Are
Edition: 1st edition
ISBN: 978-1-925452-94-5
Category: Business & Economics/Entrepreneurship/Personal Development

The stories and opinions in this book reflect the author's recollection of events
and personal way of working. Some specific names, locations, and identifying
characteristics have been changed to protect the privacy of those depicted.

Dialogue and some encounters or experiences have been recreated from the
author's memory. This book deals with personal growth and purpose and isn't a
substitute for professional advice in relation to one's mental health or psychological
issues. The information provided in this book is designed to provide helpful
information on the subjects discussed using the author's personal experiences.
This book is not meant to be used, nor should it be used, to diagnose or treat any
physical, emotional, or psychological medical condition. This book is about making
personal choices and being responsible for your actions and results, and is not a
source for treating any medical problem or condition. Always consult your own
professional health expert for advice regarding your mental or emotional health.

The publisher and author are not responsible for any specific health or psychological
needs and are not liable for any damages or negative consequences from any
treatment, action, application, or preparation to any person reading or following the
information in this book. References are provided for informational purposes only
and do not constitute endorsement of any websites or other sources. Neither the
publisher nor the individual author(s) shall be liable for any physical, psychological,
emotional, financial, or commercial damages, including, but not limited to, special,
incidental, consequential, or other damages. Our views and rights are the same: you
are responsible for your own choices, actions, and results.

I wish to dedicate this book to only a few important people in my life who are close to my heart, and who were there to support and believe in me, which has helped me become the person I am today. Without you all, I don't know where I would have ended up.

To my mother, Debbie Hansen, who taught me not to complain in life when things get tough, to never cut corners to get ahead, and to always do what's right, even when things are hard. Even though, at times, when things did get hard, you felt like you gave up on me, you never did, even when the world did. You knew when it was the right time to let go so I could find my way in my own time. Lastly, for buying one of my first life-changing books, *Rich Dad Poor Dad* by Robert Kiyosaki, which sparked a passion for accumulating knowledge.

To my partner, Petra Valachova, soon to be Petra Hansen, mother of our daughter, Zara Hansen, who has been on my crazy entrepreneurial journey of running multiple companies, chasing new businesses when I say this is the 'last one', and being caught up in building and developing property projects that take up all our resources. For letting me work late nights, long days, and continuing to study while keeping our household under control and ensuring our family remains a priority when my mind is off in the clouds.

To my children (future children included), Zara Hansen, who has shown me a whole new meaning to life, love, and happiness. For helping me understand how to be selfless and know there's more to life than my own when it's over. What I must give the world starts with you in my mind and heart. I wish you the most happiness and love in your life, and I look forward to seeing you grow into an amazing person. I hope the values, support, beliefs, and knowledge I pass on to you help you become a better person than I could ever possibly be.

CONTENTS

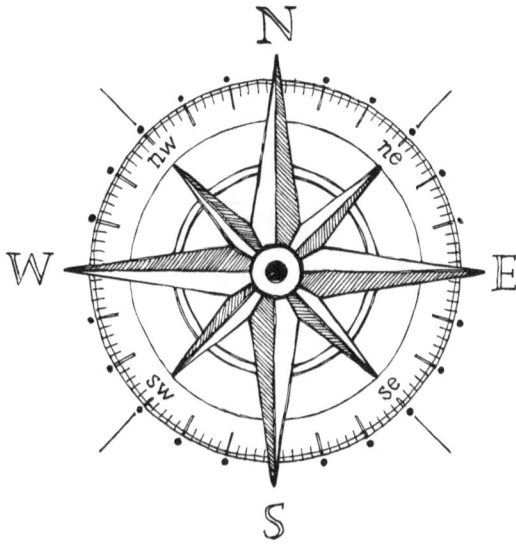

THE MOMENT
IT ALL CHANGED

From the moment I stepped foot in John's cliffside mansion, overlooking the ocean at Dover Heights, I knew I'd found a new and exciting path to wealth and success. Without a high school education, I hadn't got far on the old straight and narrow. Shitty job after shitty job had beaten me down so far I didn't know which way was up anymore, but finally I'd found another path, a path that made sense.

Big houses, flashy cars, model girlfriends – who wouldn't want that? In fact, why didn't I think of it sooner?

Fuck the straight and narrow. Where has that got me so far? Nowhere. Absolutely nowhere. I'm tired of kicking shit in life, barely earning enough to put food in the fridge. I deserve more, and now I know how to get it.

* * *

"Ricky's been shot."

"Fuck, is he –"

"Twice. One in the head, one in the neck."

"So he's –"

"He's been stabbed too."

"Wait, they shot *and* stabbed him?"

"Several times. Look, it was a bit touch and go there for a minute. He died on the table –"

"Shit"

"It's all good, they brought him back. He'll be out of action for a while, but they reckon he'll be all right."

"Finally, some good news. What happened? Do we know who did it, or why?"

"Take a guess."

"Who would – oh, fuck." *Could I be next?*

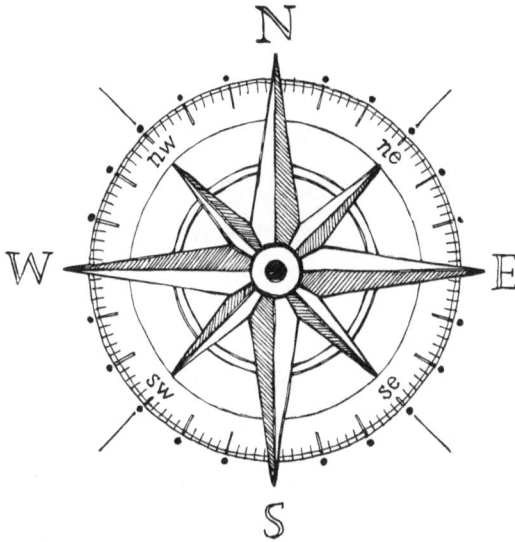

CHAPTER 1

A LESS THAN GENTLE UPBRINGING

I won't try to convince you I was the most hard done by kid in Australia – because I wasn't. Not by a long shot. But while I wasn't the poorest kid on the block, I wasn't born with a silver spoon in my mouth either. We went without in many respects. We never had the shiny, new thing, but we always had enough, and there were always presents under the tree at Christmas time. Before my parents' divorce, I'd say we were a pretty average Aussie family. After they split up, well, let's just say life got a little tougher.

Dad was a truck driver, who worked night shift five to six days a week, so he wasn't home much, and if he was, well, he was asleep. He already had two sons before he married Mum. With her, he had three more. So, for my father, I was the last of five boys. My sister came along later, but we'll get to that eventually.

As the youngest boy, I was at the bottom of the food chain. In our house, it was survival of the fittest, and every day was a fight. We fought over a lot – TV, toys, even orange juice – but often I was just fighting to be heard.

When my parents were together, we were relatively stable financially. We weren't living it up by any stretch of the imagination, but I don't recall much of a struggle. However, when Dad left, everything slowly went to shit, not just due to the loss of the financial support he provided but for many other reasons too. You'll understand soon enough.

The day he walked out the door, I knew something was wrong, but I didn't understand exactly what was happening. As a 5-year-old kid, I didn't fully grasp how relationships worked. I didn't know *why* Dad was leaving; I just knew he wouldn't be living with us anymore. There were a lot of tears. Was I capable of understanding the situation at that age? I don't know. But the problem was, no one ever sat me down and even tried to explain it. One minute, Dad was living with us; then, without explanation, he was gone. Divorce isn't uncommon, and I know a lot of kids have been in the same situation, left in the dark, not knowing what's happening or why. Parents – talk to your kids. They're often a lot more switched-on than we give them credit for. At the very least, they'll know that you tried.

As a single mother with three boys, Mum had to get creative and stretch every dollar as far as possible. We ate a lot of beef mince because she could buy it in bulk and feed us all on a budget. But here's where Mum's creativity really came into play: she had a cookbook called *100 Ways to Cook Beef Mince*. Rissoles, tacos, spaghetti bolognaise, meatloaf – you name it; she cooked it. When trying to fill our plates, potatoes and rice went a long way too. Although we were eating an abnormal amount of mince by anyone's standards, we were always well-fed and had a roof over our heads. To her credit, Mum worked hard to make sure we never went without the essentials.

To this day, I get excited whenever my partner cooks a big beef mince dish. She reckons I eat too much, so she cooks in bulk, and a big pot usually keeps me going for a few days. Do you think I get sick of it? Not a chance. Even though I'm making good money now, I love the low-cost lifestyle. Besides, when she cooks fancier dishes, half the time they don't fill me up. So, give me a big bowl of beef mince spag bol, and I'll polish it off any day of the week – and I won't complain, because I know what it's like to survive on a shoestring budget. I know people are out there right now doing it a lot tougher than I was. The struggle is real. We often take the simple things in life for granted – food, water, even having shelter over our heads!

Being the youngest of the boys, I got all the hand-me-downs: second-hand shoes, clothes, everything. I rarely had anything new after Dad left. It's not like I had to wear a potato sack to school, but I wasn't winning any fashion awards. Also, growing up, there was a biscuit factory at the end of our street – Players Biscuits – and Mum would buy the imperfect, damaged biscuits in bulk at a 50 percent, or more, discount, which was a classic way to save money. There was nothing wrong with the biscuits; they all tasted the same, but the cheap ones were usually chipped or broken. We didn't care. We were just happy to have something nice to eat. Everything we bought, we bought in bulk, or we were at least smart about it. The key was to stretch the budget as far as possible for the maximum volume of food. We also never went on holidays – how could we? We just got used to living off the essentials and forgoing even the most common luxuries. It was forced budgeting, and, to us, it was life.

Nowadays, people who might not have been doing it tough in the past are experiencing the same forced budgeting. They really have to pay attention to where their money is going. High interest rates and the rising cost of living (inflation pressures) can put a squeeze on anyone's budget, and people have to get really creative if they want to so much as eat a half-decent meal. The difference between now and then is that the cost of food wasn't so inflated. Yes, we were flat out on the mince, but we also ate a lot of veggies. We could afford the essentials... just. We never wasted any food, and we never had soft drink in the fridge. Occasionally, we did have juice, but it was usually gone before it hit the fridge. If I wanted even a taste, I'd have to fight my brothers for it. Sometimes I'd get some, sometimes not. We had it tough, but, like I said, many others are out there doing it a lot tougher right now.

Mum used to stress whenever she opened a bill. I recall these days like they were yesterday. I can see, and even feel, the pressure she was under, the stress she felt when her eyes met the unfolded A4 page showing AMOUNT OVERDUE. Would this be the one that tipped us over the edge? Somehow, she made it work, usually making it to payday with little more than $5, $6, $7, or, if we were lucky, $8 in the bank. Even in the early 90s, that was barely any money.

When I started making money, the budgeting mindset stuck with me in a way. Yes, I bought a car when I was young, went to concerts, and went out drinking, but I never really went over-the-top with my spending. There's a certain reassurance that comes with knowing you could live on a tight budget if you needed to. I could go back to eating mince meals every day and only drinking orange juice on special occasions if the situation required it. Do I want to? Fuck no. I love the freedom money provides but if the shit hit the fan and I was *forced* to stretch every dollar as far as possible, I'd suck it up and make it work. Why? Because I've done it before, and I know how to focus myself. If I do get into financial trouble, I know I have the discipline, not to mention the muscle memory, to do what's necessary to pull myself out of it. Hey, I could be wrong. Maybe I've grown too comfortable now and wouldn't be able to handle all the sacrifices I'd need to make. Perhaps I've grown too accustomed to the luxuries of life.

For instance, would I be able to surrender my morning coffee? Here's hoping we never have to find out.

When I did start making money, because I was reserved with my spending, I was able to generate a strong surplus, and fast. Without a surplus, you can't do much, right? Really, you can't do anything impactful with *zero* dollars to spare. It's a simple maths equation. So, as I started to make money, I kept the luxuries to a minimum and held plenty of savings in the bank for a rainy day. Eventually, as I became more financially savvy, it was investments that gave me security and peace of mind, as I knew I had a backup if the unforeseen happened. I'm bringing this up now because it's a problem I see over and over again.

People start making more money, so they start spending more money. Frequently, I see clients with joint household incomes of $300K or more, and they have no surplus. Yes, I know it's hard to believe that some people earn $300K, $600K, or more in annual wages. I never believed it myself, but once you're around it and start to see what's actually possible, it can spark something in your mind. It's a window of proof that it can be done. With those clients, their expenses practically outweigh their earnings, and I'm baffled every time. *What on Earth are you doing?* You can't build wealth and freedom if you're spending all of your disposable income on luxuries and a lavish lifestyle. But they didn't start spending that much on day one. It's a silent wealth killer that creeps in gradually. Often, you don't even know it's happening. People tend to adjust their lifestyles over time, and then they become comfortable and complacent where they are. It's a great way to get stuck in the same position for 40, 45, even 50 years, a slave to your work and the system. Forced budgeting is easy in that sense – because you're *forced* to do it. Try persuading someone with a six-figure income that they don't need a new car every three to five years and they should slow down on the overseas holidays and new clothes, or they don't deserve to move from their three-bedroom house to a five-bedroom with a pool. Not living in poverty is great, but you still need to be realistic with your spending. You still need to budget. With the right approach, you could go from well-off to living like a king, but it won't happen without discipline, and it won't happen overnight. It comes at a cost, and that cost is: sacrifice + time applied = results (from the accumulation of good decisions and budgeting).

Some clients are genuinely overstretched with their financial commitments. For example, they might have three kids and a mortgage and aren't spending their earnings on anything too crazy. They're working full-time but living at their financial threshold. My advice to them? You need to make more money. Trust me, it's not something people want to hear. As we know, it's not so easy to just make more money or increase your income. I understand the struggle. But what alternative do you have? Would you rather be destined to a life of servitude, slaving away at your job, losing a big chunk of your income to tax, maybe having a little left over when you retire at age 67? Hopefully, your health is still good so you can actually enjoy your retirement. Yep, this is the standard the system says is okay. Well, to me and my clients, it's not okay. They deserve more; you deserve more; we *all* deserve more, and there are changes you can make to create the life you want. The good news – it requires less effort than you might think.

When I tell clients they need to make more money, it means

they need to ask for a pay rise, charge more per hour, upskill themselves, whatever it takes. Essentially, they've got to take action to put themselves in a better position. They've got to make themselves more valuable. If you can't ditch the mortgage, the three kids, and the two cars, the money has to come from somewhere else. If you don't start generating a surplus to invest, to grow a business, to build some wealth, or to have extra to pay into a mortgage or savings account, you'll be another victim taken by the system. You'll be stuck living on that threshold until you retire, half-broke and burnt out. We don't want that, do we? Of course not! Who would want to have a hard life with limited money to live off and enjoy? Why not live a great life instead? With the right strategies in place, you can.

For example, if you earn $100,000 p.a. (per annum, that is, per year) in Australia, you pay around $27,000 p.a. in income tax, so you have a net (after tax) income of around $73,000 p.a. If you need more money but can't quickly increase your income, start a business, or get a pay rise, then understanding how to effectively use tax reduction strategies is crucial.

In Australia, our government allows you to reduce your income tax if you borrow to invest or just invest in assets like property and shares. With the right creative thinking and knowledge of the tax system, you can still earn $100,000 p.a. while reducing your tax bill to, say, $17,000 p.a., making your new net income $83,000 p.a. That's a $10,000 after tax increase to your surplus, which is pretty insane when you think about it. It makes you wonder why more people aren't doing it – and that's just the tax benefits. What about the investment and returns you'll be accumulating or generating?

Compare this to asking for a pay rise at work on a $100,000 p.a. salary. If your employer gives you an above-average pay rise of, say, 5 percent, you'd have an extra $5,000 p.a. but after tax, it would only be around $3,275 p.a. additional net income, which is around $62.98 per week. This small pay rise is unlikely to have a significant impact on your situation. Of course, that doesn't mean you shouldn't ask for a pay rise, but you should also consider other ways to increase your net income. The more, the better. Generating as much net income as possible is a key component of making your dream lifestyle a reality.

Essentially, the system has rules, tricks, and loopholes that anyone can utilise, and understanding them is more powerful, more beneficial than wishful thinking, hoping for a pay rise that actually makes an impact. Almost anyone can start using these tricks today. If you're not ready right now, you may only be 3, 6, or 12 months away from putting the right structures in place to get you there. Once you gain momentum, the sky's the limit.

Anyway, where were we? Growing up, we didn't have any luxuries, but it wasn't by choice. We still did sport; we always had bikes, and, honestly, we didn't miss out on the things that mattered. However, I gradually began to notice that we didn't have what other families had. I didn't have what my friend, Jon the Greek, had.

JON THE GREEK AND A GLIMPSE OF THE GOOD LIFE

Seeing how Jon's family lived was the biggest indicator that I wasn't exactly living an upper-class lifestyle. While *we* never had soft drink in the fridge, Jon's family practically had it on tap. The fridge in the garage was chock-full of cans, which they bought in blocks of 24. I'd never seen anything like it. To them, it was normal. To me, it was liquid gold.

But it was more than just soft drink that set Jon's family apart. They had a really nice house, the newest PlayStation, a jet ski, and expensive mountain bikes. Basically, they could buy anything they wanted. Well, as a kid, it felt that way. It wasn't a reality I was used to, but I was beginning to realise what was possible outside our family environment.

If the name 'Jon the Greek' didn't give it away, Jon and his family were Greek, and they had that work-hard mentality that many immigrants have. While they were hard workers, Jon's dad was also a smart worker in the sense that he had a highly skilled occupation: he worked in IT. Now, we're talking the early 90s here, when computers were still somewhat mysterious and IT wasn't a career many people considered, let alone pursued. So, not only did Jon's dad work hard, but his skill set was highly sought after, which meant he could make a lot more money than the average, unskilled worker. When you combine a strong work ethic with a valuable skill set, frankly, you've set yourself up for long-term success. When it comes to choosing a career – not that everyone gets that luxury – it's definitely something to consider. *Is my profession in demand? Am I willing to work hard to build my skill set and be a stand-out in my field? Can I use those skills to generate wealth and create financial freedom?* I'm not saying you shouldn't follow your passion, but a passion doesn't always pay the bills. You've also got to be realistic.

Jon's family had a good culture, a good *structure*. His mum worked part-time, so she was around quite a bit. My mum, on the other hand, could only be around for the bare minimum. She did, after all, have a family to support on her own, so she worked as much as she could, working as a receptionist at the local RSL. At night, Jon's family would all sit around the dinner table, something we, as a family, rarely did. His dad, sitting there in his corporate attire, would discuss business ideas, such as washing cars or mowing lawns on weekends and after school, with us kids. He'd also discuss the computer industry, which few people knew anything about at the time, and, importantly, stressed the value of hard work.

As a kid, I never had that level of structure at home, even before the divorce. Because Dad was away so often, working night shift, we never got to sit down for those family dinners and deep conversations. It was just another thing Jon's family had that mine didn't. See, it wasn't just the material things we missed out on but also the less tangible, but no less important, family moments. Like I said, we never went on family holidays because they weren't a necessity. The budget just wouldn't allow it. Instead, I spent most school holidays at home, running amuck with my brothers. I'm not complaining – they were good times – but I did notice the difference between us and other families. I did, however, go on one trip with Jon and his family to Nelson Bay, which gave me further insight into how well-off they were. Not only could they afford to take themselves on a holiday, but they could afford to take me too. When I say Jon and his family were well-off, I mean they *seemed* well-off to me at the time. From the perspective of a kid in a single-mother, four-child, lower-class family, they were *loaded*. However, in reality, they were probably earning just above average income. Essentially, they were middle-class. It's all about perspective. Looking back from the position I'm in now, I realise they probably weren't as well-off as I thought.

Later, at age 27, I took my family to the snow during the winter, which was about a five-hour drive south of Sydney. When we got there, I realised it was our first family holiday since my parents' divorce… 22 years later. It took us a while, but we finally got there. Through the rules and lessons I learnt over the years, I was able to beat the odds, create the life I wanted, and share my success with my family. How did I do it? We'll get to that later.

Fortunately, Mum pretty much owned the house we lived in. She had managed to pay Dad out before he took off to live in another state, so we weren't being squeezed by a big mortgage or rent, which helped Mum hold on to our family home. She still lives there to this day. At one point, when things got tough in a big way, she did have to refinance and draw more money out of the house. We'll get to that soon.

Where I grew up near Cronulla, it was mostly a middle- to upper-class demographic, so, even though we were struggling, we didn't live in a poor neighbourhood. Back then, if both parents were together and worked hard, they could do all right for themselves. Times have definitely changed. As a truck driver, Dad earned pretty good money, which was why they managed to pay off the house in a reasonable amount of time. However, he traded large amounts of his time to earn that money, working night shifts, away from his family, which might have contributed to my parents' failed marriage. It's quite an ironic outcome that, as a provider, you can work hard for long hours to provide for the family you love and, at the same time, negatively impact your marriage. The result? You end up separated from the same family you worked so hard to support.

I don't think Dad even realised the marriage was falling apart. By his account, he was shocked when Mum proposed a divorce. He has since made a point to remind me that she waited until *after* they owned the house to kick him out. In these situations, no one wins, which is probably why no result or compromise ever seems perfect to both parties in a failing marriage. Back then, the gap between an average household income and median house price was a lot smaller than it is today. For a lot of families, home ownership wasn't so far out of reach. If at least one person could work and earn a decent wage, they could live fairly comfortably. Like I said, times have changed but if you don't change with them and create a solid plan to obtain financial freedom, which may include owning your own home, you're in for a tough ride.

House Price Index to Median Household Income

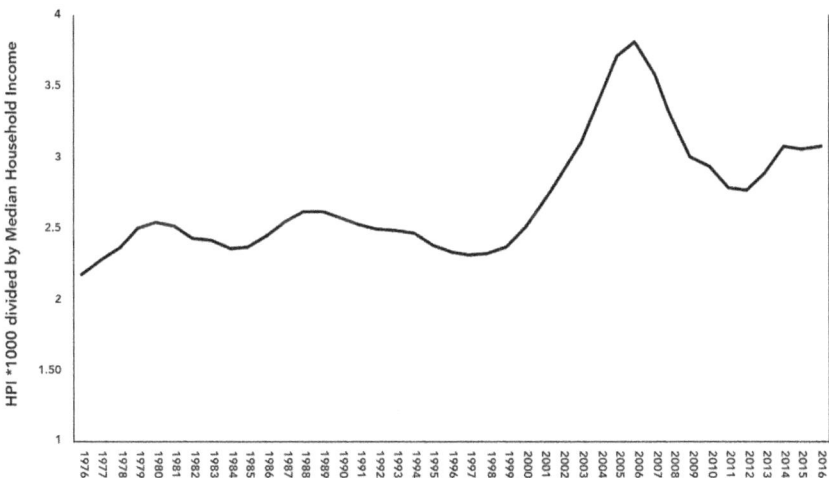

Relationship between average income and median house prices over time.

Even in those days, single parents had it tough. While Mum tried to work as much as she could, she couldn't work full-time because she had a group of boys running amuck at home. When she was at home, she was forced to wear several different hats – cook, chauffeur, cleaner, handyman, mediator, father – because she didn't have the support of another parent. It was a battle, but Mum always kept it together and made ends meet, living by fair, honest values and never complaining. Thanks to her, and to Dad for paying off the house – thanks, Dad! – we always had a roof over our heads, which I'm grateful for. To pay Dad out after the split, Mum did have to refinance the house, but the mortgage wasn't huge, so we scraped by.

Ultimately, Jon's family gave me a taste of what was possible. Poverty wasn't the only option. If I worked hard, got the right job, and played it smart, I could have a fridge full of soft drink too, and bulk beef mince meals would become optional. If I ever wanted to treat myself, I could go for a big, juicy steak instead. I began to realise there could be more to life than second-hand shoes and mincemeat dinners. Jon's dad had direction; he had *drive*. He knew what he wanted, and, importantly, he knew what he had to do to get it. He showed me what success could look like.

Look, while we didn't take family holidays or splurge on other luxuries, we still had it pretty good. Compared to a lot of people, I actually had a great childhood. However, nothing great ever lasts, and tougher times were on the horizon.

THE PROBLEM WITH OUR SCHOOL SYSTEM (DON'T GET ME STARTED...)

At around 7:30 am, one morning before school, I woke up to the sound of sirens. Was it police or ambulance? I didn't know, but emergency vehicles were fairly common in our street, as it was a main road with a lot of passing traffic, so I didn't think much of it at first. But something was different about this morning. The sirens weren't getting fainter, as they normally did. Instead, they got louder. It was almost as if they were right outside the house...

A heavy knock sounded on the front door, followed by rapid footsteps in the hallway. Men in white shirts ran past my bedroom door, headed for Mum's room. I followed, with no idea what was happening or why these people were in our house. I didn't know it at the time, but my world was about to collapse. Mum had suffered major blood loss. Thankfully, she survived, but the diagnosis wasn't good. Cancer, they said. She had a long battle ahead of her, and, as a kid of only 10 years old, I had a lot of unanswered questions stacking up inside me.

Mum was a very straitlaced lady. She barely drank back then, and she stopped drinking completely after the cancer. She didn't smoke or have many, or really any, unhealthy habits and, at the time, was only in her mid-40s. So, when she got sick, it shocked everyone. It was completely out of her control and couldn't have happened at a worse time.

Financially, we were still struggling, but we always had food on the table – Mum made sure of that. When she got sick, there was a lot of uncertainty, and we all started to feel the pressure. As a kid, you can only understand so much, and you can only express so much. It doesn't help when you're always left in the dark about what's going on.

Until high school, I'd been a good student. I paid attention, didn't disrupt the class, was in the higher levels throughout my school years, and got really good grades across all academic areas. I was particularly good at maths, and I enjoyed learning, trying to understand how things worked, and solving complex problems. Sure, I got into some trouble here and there, but, for the most part, I was focused and well-behaved. However, Mum's diagnosis derailed everything, especially school. The divorce had been hard, but, as a family, we'd kept it together. At times, we struggled financially, but we were mostly all right. However, when Mum got sick, it all fell apart, not just financially – our entire home environment went to ruin. Mum, the person who held everything together, was suddenly struggling with her health, without explanation. During this time, I had a lot of bottled-up emotions and unspoken questions, and I expressed my confusion and frustration through violence and acting out. I was scared of losing my mother, and I wanted to avoid that fear at all costs. Let me give you some context around what I mean by 'violence' and 'acting out'.

In a house full of young boys, with little parental supervision due to our single mother working to keep us fed and clothed, we had to develop our own social system, a way of dealing with problems. If there was a dispute among us boys, we solved it with physical actions, not words, not communication; there was no emotional intelligence involved. To put it bluntly, we settled our disputes with violence. Really, we didn't know any other way. The problem was, after Mum's diagnosis, I took the same approach at school.

The school I attended was a specialised sports high school, which took on kids from all over Sydney, so the student body consisted of over 1200 teenagers from different cultural backgrounds and nationalities from across the city. The school was quite rough, and the combination of big, fit kids and a diverse range of nationalities created some heated moments. Day to day, there was a lot of conflict.

If someone gave me shit at school, well, I didn't have the emotional intelligence to talk it through, and I had a back-against-the-wall mentality. I'm sure you can imagine how most situations played out. Combine suppressed emotions with puberty levels of testosterone and a rough school, and you've got a recipe for trouble. Most of the time, I was getting into fights with bigger, older kids after standing up for myself. On the surface, it may have looked like I was fearless, but really I was afraid of the world, afraid of being hurt. Standing up for myself, fighting to solve my problems made me feel safer. Yes, it was a destructive outer projection of my inner pain, but it was all I knew how to do.

Of course, the teachers didn't approve of my methods, but they didn't understand what was happening with me, and they didn't know how to handle a kid with suppressed emotions and destructive coping mechanisms. They don't really teach that sort of stuff to would-be teachers at university – at least, they didn't back then.

Personally, I didn't understand what all the fuss was about. I was so caught up in everything that was happening at home that I didn't realise my reactions weren't what most people would consider 'normal'. Like I said, it's how we dealt with problems at home. We never used words or expressed our emotions. To us, violence was the solution to most problems. If you've never experienced that type of environment, it can come as a bit of a shock to learn that some kids grow up this way. However, knowing what some kids are going through helps us understand why some people grow up broken. Like me, they may not have learnt how to express themselves or deal with their emotions in a healthy way. When someone doesn't understand their emotions, how can they properly communicate what they're experiencing?

To me, my behaviour was normal, sad but true. To others, I was a violent kid who could turn around and clock someone at any moment. In their eyes, I was a delinquent. You could say I was feared, but, like I said, I was scared myself, scared that the world would see me for what I was – lost, broken, confused. Violence was my protection, my armour against letting anyone in. I'm sure you've heard the age-old question: Are we the products of nature or nurture? As far as I'm concerned, we're born with unique personalities; however, our environments and life experiences have a massive influence on who we become as we mature. In my mind, I couldn't show any vulnerability because, at home, I'd learnt that doing so was a sign of weakness, and the consequences were pain and suffering. So, I pushed my emotions aside and committed to the tough-guy act.

"You don't hit people," my teachers would say when I got in fights at school.

"Really? What do you do?" I'd ask because I had no other tools for expressing my feelings, and I didn't know how to protect myself.

"You talk to them, avoid confrontation, walk away, or tell them you don't like what they said. Tell them how they made you feel, and that what they said was hurtful. You can do this in a nice way."

Ha! Could you imagine if I'd said to my brothers, "Can I *please* have a glass of orange juice? It's not very nice when you drink it all and leave me nothing, because I'd like some too." They would have punched me harder. In my environment, words didn't work; you had to use your fists to be heard, at least this was what I believed for many years. If you wanted orange juice, to watch TV, anything, you fought for it, plain and simple. Not so simple in the real world though, right? Saying all that, there was a lot of brotherly love between us, and, honestly, we had a fairly good upbringing. We still played sport and got along well for the most part. We just had a way of problem-solving that didn't resonate with society at large. So, by doing what I knew, I got labelled the naughty kid with anger issues, essentially being categorised as the 'trouble child'.

Due to my behaviour, the school system put me on a red card, which teachers used to rate my behaviour each day and give me a ranking. I was constantly tracked, monitored, and labelled, which only increased the pressure and magnified belief in the delinquent archetype I was becoming. The red card unquestionably marked me as the naughty kid. It also meant that, if my score was too low, I lost a lot of my student privileges, such as attending school discos and excursions and playing sports. Ultimately, all the red card really did was create extra, unnecessary pressure. Clearly, I was far from perfect – I *was* troubled – but none of the school's methods identified or addressed the underlying reasons for my behaviour.

At school, I was in constant conflict with teachers, and I frequently felt singled out. Yes, if they didn't take action, I would have disrupted the other students, but the teachers weren't trained to deal with the types of behavioural issues I had. On top of that, they had 20 other kids to teach and couldn't give me the attention I needed. Even now, many schools are understaffed, and the teachers are overworked and underpaid. They do a difficult but essential job, and I have the utmost respect for all the teachers out there who are doing their best.

After the cancer diagnosis, my brothers, aged 13 and 15, my baby sister, who was only a few months old, and I all got split up, living with friends and relatives for several months while Mum received treatment. Being in high school, the disruption was tough to handle. The jump from primary school to high school can be difficult at the best of times. In the previous year, you were a senior student. Suddenly, you're in an environment where most of the kids are older and bigger than you. Being among the youngest in that type of situation comes with a lot of societal pressure, and most kids are just doing their best to fit in. Unfortunately, my way of fitting in was to fight people who pissed me off. At that age, we're becoming little adults, with hormones and emotions – it's a lot to deal with, even without what I was going through.

With the divorce, the diagnosis, and the overall disruption, I had so much going on inside my head. I didn't know how to communicate what I was feeling with words, so I used my fists. My problem – one of many – was that I couldn't just walk away. If someone said the wrong thing to me, or even to someone else, and I felt it was a bullying situation, I was too stubborn to let it go. I couldn't just shut my mouth, and it would always end in a fight, which meant another visit to the principal's office. See, I thought I was saving others as well as standing up for myself and making my point. Essentially, I was standing up for what I believed in, which was great, but, while my intent was good, my methods were far from ideal. There are better ways to make a point. Regardless of my intent or actions, I was still labelled the naughty kid.

Academically, I could have been a top student, and I was initially put into the top classes. However, I was too disruptive, so I was pigeonholed as a troublemaker, nothing more, even though I had the capacity to learn and do well in school. The problem was, I only excelled when I could actually focus and apply myself, which was something I struggled with, often disrupting others and bringing them down with me. As a kid, I was fairly hyperactive, so I'd power through my work, and, when I'd finished, I'd start talking to other students. Basically, I was being disruptive on purpose because I was bored. Eventually, I was required to sit right at the front of the classroom during every lesson, before I'd even done anything wrong. Did it help? No way. "That's discrimination!" I'd yell. It just gave me another thing to argue about with the teachers. I was being picked on, singled out. I was the victim, and things were unjust; they were *wrong*. Where were my rights?!

Now, as an adult, I can look back and realise I had very little clue what was going on. I was a confused, hurt, broken little boy who didn't know how to become a man. Was I right back then? Definitely not, but I also wasn't being heard or understood, so I responded by acting like a little shit. I was rebellious, argumentative, and outspoken, and I didn't agree with the politics of the school or the outdated education system.

"Face the front."

"Open your textbook."

"Sit still."

"Read this."

"Write that."

"Don't question it."

I felt that I had a good reason for acting the way I did. The issue was that I didn't know how to control or use my thoughts, feelings, and opinions in a more constructive way. Instead, I took a destructive approach.

It also didn't help that one of my brothers, Daniel, who was two years older than me, had gone to the same school and been kicked out just a few weeks after I started. We looked a little alike, and the teachers started mistaking me for him from day one, using his name in place of mine. I practically had a black mark against me from the start. Granted, my behaviour didn't help, but, as a confused kid with shit going on at home, it felt like the school had it in for me and had written me off as too hard to fix. I was the outcast, the problem kid, and it seemed like I wasn't worth the effort or attention.

One of the biggest problems was that the teachers didn't talk *to* me; they talked *at* me. No one ever sat me down to ask what was going on. If they had, they would have learnt that my dad had left, my mum was sick, and I didn't fully understand what was happening. I don't blame the teachers. Many of them were, and still are, overworked and underpaid, and they didn't have the time or resources to sort through some kid's home life. I'm not bagging out the school system or those who work within it, but it doesn't cater for every student. It certainly didn't cater for a kid full of confusion, frustration, and pain. At home, among my brothers, I'd been at the bottom of the food chain for so long. I was used to having to fight for what I wanted, so that's what I did. I fought, and I argued, and I kept everything bottled up, never having the ability to speak up about the battle I was fighting within.

The words that aren't spoken are the most painful, dangerous, and destructive to us all. I can't stress enough that we need to open up, communicate more, and encourage our children, friends, and family around us to talk. Even if you think your fears, worries, and problems are stupid or not worth discussing, discuss them anyway, as holding on to them for too long is detrimental to the mind and body. Would a conversation have straightened out my behaviour entirely and made me a perfect, straight-A student? Probably not, but I might have learnt how to deal with stress in a social environment at a much younger age and been able to better navigate some of the challenges I faced as a young adult growing up.

In less than two years of high school, I racked up 11 suspensions. In my second year, I probably spent more time at home suspended than attending school, which was a whole new problem. Because Mum worked during the day, I'd be home alone, which meant I could go out and meet up with all the other naughty kids who weren't at school. Did they not think it through before they suspended me? Likely not. I doubt they even knew Mum wouldn't be at home. I doubt they even asked.

Mum still remembers me coming home from school complaining about the school system, the academics, the rules, the structure, and the authority the teachers wield over all the kids. I often told her I'd never become an employee, someone who just follows an employer, works 40–50 hours a week, does whatever they're told, gets a capped wage, and waits to use their four weeks of annual leave a year after working 48 weeks straight. That sort of life wasn't for me at all; I didn't fit that mould, and I knew this after only two years of high school.

I didn't want to spend another ten years of my life finishing high school and then going to university, all the while memorising and reciting dry, rigid details from textbooks. What an absolute joke! How can they expect the textbooks to have all the answers? When I was at school, all the tests focused on assessing how well we could learn and retain information, without questioning any of it, without thinking outside the pages of the assigned textbooks. If we could adequately demonstrate our ability to recite all the appropriate facts, we would earn a good mark and be free to enter the outside world as a qualified adult and pursue our dreams. What a load of crap.

Look, once again, I'm not trying to disrespect the teachers or the people within the school system who dedicate their lives to helping teach and develop our children. They do an amazing job, but I realised early on that the system was flawed. It didn't make sense to me. In my experience, discussing problems and debating solutions wasn't encouraged. We weren't taught to think outside the box and come up with novel ideas. Anyone who questioned the status quo or the approved material was immediately shut down, something I experienced a lot. I constantly argued with teachers about the school system and how it didn't cater to everyone. I saw the flaws, and I wanted things to change, but I didn't know how to communicate my ideas and opinions constructively, so I was simply labelled disruptive and told to stop arguing. If they had bothered to look below the surface, they would have seen that I was passionate about fixing the broken system so people like me don't get left behind, thinking they aren't as smart as the other kids because they can't – or don't want to – memorise and apply rigid textbook knowledge. And don't even get me started on the exams… One test can dictate whether a student passes or fails a subject, and it all comes down to how well they're able to memorise the approved information. It's no wonder so many teenagers are anxious and depressed in modern societies all over the world. While social pressure is one factor, the pressure to perform also has a negative impact. When kids believe they need to achieve a certain mark to be successful and they fall short, they feel like they've failed and their lives can only go nowhere. Well, let me tell you now – that's bullshit. How do I know? I've been there, failing miserably in school but succeeding in life today. The same outcome is possible for anyone who's willing to take meaningful action to reach their goals.

I'm sure there are a lot of people who feel like they don't fit into the school system – and I don't blame them. Plenty of people struggle with academics but end up being successful out in the real world because, let's face it, school isn't the real world. It's a small portion of your overall life that helps build the foundations for learning and discipline, but it's definitely not designed with different learning styles, abilities, and thought processes in mind. Generally, school doesn't teach you the skills you need to survive outside its walls. We need to understand that there's more than one way to achieve what we want in life. I don't need to be a model student to bring something meaningful to the world, and neither do you. Steve Jobs, Richard Branson, and former US president Harry Truman were all college dropouts who went on to do great things. For some, school works, but it failed me. Some of us fall through the cracks and once we start falling, it's difficult to stop.

THAT'S A FACT

Emotional intelligence (aka EQ) is a bigger performance indicator than IQ. What's EQ? Basically, EQ is a measurement of your ability to understand your emotions and those of others. People with high EQ scores are not only top performers, but they also make good leaders, which makes sense, right?[1] When it comes to managing teams, book smarts only get you so far. To be successful, you've got to be able to relate to people on an emotional level. Imagine trying to build a big, successful business… You can't do it alone, and the better you can recruit and empower others, the more scalable your business will be. Even in a small business, the more you adapt to your customers, the more aligned and relatable you'll be.

So, if you've ever thought, *This academic shit isn't for me,* it doesn't mean you can't win at life. Let's be honest – you're probably not going to win a Nobel prize in physics or anything like that but if you've got a decent EQ level, you can still be a leader, an entrepreneur, an artist, whatever it is you're drawn to.

As an indicator of success, street smarts (non-traditional learnings and thinking) trump book smarts almost every time. Beyond the average IQ level, the IQ-success correlation declines.[2] Essentially, we see diminishing returns. However, when it comes to EQ, more really is more, with high EQ being a strong indicator of success in many areas of life.[3]

When I wasn't allowed at school due to being suspended, I spent most of my days hanging out with housing commission kids or other kids from single-parent or disruptive homes, smoking, drinking, experimenting with pot – basically, getting into more trouble. But what else was I supposed to do?

When you're a 14-year-old kid smoking in the streets on a Tuesday in the middle of the day, people get suspicious. Often, the cops would pull up and ask why we weren't in school and if our parents knew we were there, that sort of thing. We never got arrested or in any real trouble, but the police were filing reports, which eventually got me put into the care of the PCYC (Police Citizens Youth Club) to try to get me onto the right path.

In the late 90s, the NSW government launched a program called the Young Offenders Act, which aimed to rehabilitate delinquent teens. By helping young people create good behaviours and make better choices early on in life, the hope was that they wouldn't end up in the system as adults. However, the program wasn't just about helping teens; it was also about saving money in the long term. Keeping people in prison isn't cheap. Adult incarceration costs taxpayers a significant amount of money each year, and that figure is constantly growing. The idea was, if spending money on rehabilitating delinquent teens kept them out of prison as adults, it was money well spent. It was sound logic, and the program had a massive impact on my life, which I'll discuss in more detail later.

Eventually, the school system was done chewing me up, so it spat me out, and I was expelled from all state schools in New South Wales. They told me I was uncontrollable and too disruptive to the school and the other students. Was I really that bad? If so, how did I get that way? When we're born, we're blank canvases. A baby doesn't come out of the womb wanting to start arguments and fight people. Or do they? Along the way, my canvas got painted, and the picture was one of rebellion, belligerence, and a willingness to fight for any cause. Whether I was wrong or right in those fights, I couldn't accept something that I felt was unfair, so I refused to back down from any arguments. Simply put, I was too much for the teachers to handle. In an underfunded and under-resourced system, they didn't have the time or the tools to deal with me, so they kicked me out. The simplest solution. Out of sight, out of mind. Don't get me wrong, I would have been a handful to manage and teach, so I'm sure they felt like they had no other choice.

In this country, we get free education, which I'm grateful for, and our schools provide an invaluable service to the community. However, due to my environment and the situation at home, I'd become too incompatible with the current system. I didn't fit the mould, and the teachers were ill-equipped to deal with me. In their defence, I believe they did everything they could with the resources they had, and, in hindsight, expelling me was best for everyone.

Psychologists had a crack at trying to sort me out, diagnosing me with oppositional defiant disorder (ODD). Basically, I didn't respect authority. No shit! What an astonishing diagnosis. How do you cure something like *that*? Although Mum's health had begun to stabilise, she still wasn't 100 percent recovered from her cancer, and she couldn't handle me at that time. After being expelled from the NSW school system, I couldn't attend another state school, and I was below the legal age to leave. So, I got shipped off to Boys' Town, where everyone hoped I'd get the support and structure I needed.

WHAT'S MORE IMPORTANT, HEALTH OR WEALTH?

When Mum got sick, I saw how quickly someone's health can deteriorate. One minute, she was healthy. The next minute, she was battling a terrible disease. Like I said, she was a straitlaced lady, but it's no secret that she was under a lot of stress. Was this a contributor to her condition? I could only guess, but it wouldn't surprise me.

More and more, I've come to believe that our health is our most important asset. It's not just about looking physically fit and healthy. The health of our bodies, minds, and souls collectively needs nourishing. Having a sixpack won't solve all your problems – well, from what I've heard, anyway. Without your health, you can't have anything else. Whether you're rich or poor, health issues can haunt you and quite literally ruin your life. Whether you're successful or not, disease can strike, just like it did with Steve Jobs, one of the most successful entrepreneurs of our time. When death came calling, neither Jobs' success, wealth, or fame could save him. He died just like anyone else. Of course, when you're wealthy, looking after your health is easier. You can afford better healthcare, better food – have you seen the price of organic fruit and veggies? – and a better lifestyle in general. Most of the time, you can budget your way out of a poor financial situation. Mum proved that, and I see it proven again and again with my clients. Generally, however, you can't budget your way out of a serious health crisis. Steve Jobs certainly couldn't, and he had more money than any sane person could ever want or need.

When I was young, I didn't fully understand the value of good health, but I did intuitively know that certain actions made me feel good. For example, playing sport and going to the gym became a big outlet for me. When it felt like the world around me was falling apart, a brutal workout often helped me clear my head.

On reflection, physical activity wasn't just a way to disconnect from reality; it was also a way to boost endorphins – the feel-good chemicals in the brain – and lower stress hormones. I didn't realise it at the time, but there was biochemistry at play. All I knew then was that going to the gym relaxed me, made me feel good, so I did it. I discovered this at Boys' Town and also when attending programs at the PCYC through the Young Offenders Act. Being physically active helped me understand and release my bottled-up thoughts, emotions, and frustrations before they built up and exploded out of me in a destructive way.

THAT'S A FACT

Exercise isn't just good for the body; it's also good for the brain. When we physically exert ourselves, we lower the body's stress hormones – adrenaline and cortisol – and release endorphins, which act like pain-killers in the brain. Basically, exercise relaxes us and makes us feel good.[4]

So, if you're struggling with low mood, physical activity is a great way to boost it. The key is to find a sport or activity you enjoy, do it regularly, and make fitness a habit.

It wasn't Mum's battle with cancer that steered me towards living a relatively healthy lifestyle. While she had always looked after herself, she didn't go on a serious health kick until *after* she recovered, exposing me to the idea of creating healthy habits. At the time, I didn't realise her lifestyle change was rubbing off on me, but it was, and I've been pretty health-conscious ever since. I'm wary about eating too much processed food, too many poor-quality takeaway meals, and drinking too many sugary drinks. When you eat quality meals, your body and brain just work better. It's not always easy to eat well on a budget, I know, but it *is* possible if you get creative, like Mum did with her endless supply of mincemeat recipes.

I'm sure you've heard it all before, but, on top of eating well, we also need to make sure we're drinking enough water during the day. More than half of the human body is made up of water, so, yeah, it's pretty important for our health and survival. I usually drink a couple of litres a day, but the ideal amount varies depending on a few factors, such as how much you sweat. I've heard so many people say they don't like the taste of water. *Are they for real?* How can someone not like the taste of water? What a cop out. Unless you've got something funky going on with the pipes in your home, water doesn't really have a taste. But that's the real problem, isn't it? If you're used to getting that sugar hit from soft drink or juice, in comparison, water does taste pretty shit. However, our tastes can be changed, and you can retrain your taste buds to tolerate water – the liquid of life – and still enjoy a soft drink every now and then. It's all about cultivating a bit of discipline around what you choose to consume.

As you know, I got in a lot of fights at school, so, at age 14, when I was expelled and sent to Boys' Town, I started doing some boxing training. Not only did I learn how to fight properly, but I also practised discipline, focus, and commitment. See, when I *wanted* to do something, like boxing, I could apply myself with extreme discipline and focus but when I wasn't interested in a topic or task, like learning algebra for instance, all discipline was gone. I don't want to spend all day banging on about the flaws of the education system but if it played to kids' strengths and interests instead of taking a one-size-fits-all approach, we'd see fewer students feeling unheard, uncatered for, and discouraged from learning altogether. It's not learning that I have a problem with; it's forcing kids to learn shit they're not interested in and will never use. It's an archaic way to educate our kids, and we could do better. All right, I'm done hanging shit on the education system, for now, anyway. We're here to talk about health.

So, through observing Mum's lifestyle changes and experiencing the benefits of exercise for myself, I built some pretty good habits around health and fitness. Even now, I live a fairly active lifestyle, playing sport and getting to the gym whenever I can. If I don't regularly exercise and blow off some steam, mentally, I'm a mess. I can't function at 100 percent. The thing is, people who don't exercise don't understand how good they can feel. I'm not saying regularly hitting the gym is the magic cure for everything, but it sure as hell helps.

If I could encourage you to develop one thing in your life, it would be self-discipline. It's something you can apply to so many goals, including budgeting to save for a house deposit or to pay off your mortgage faster, or investing in and building your own business to create financial freedom. When you practise discipline and develop healthy habits and routines, reaching your goals, achieving the success you deserve, and creating overall abundance in your life becomes not only possible but also much easier. Without discipline and self-control, you'll struggle to get ahead – period!

Fortunately for me, I developed these traits and built them into my framework at a young age. If I wanted food on the table, I had to be disciplined with my spending. If I wanted to keep my internal dialogue in check and balance my body and mind, I had to be disciplined about fitness. Many of the constructive routines and behaviours I built over the years have continued throughout my adult life – I wouldn't be where I am today without them. To this day, I still rely on them as much as, if not more than, I did when I was younger. The difference now is I'm more aware of how important discipline, routine, and healthy habits are for my mind and body so I can continue to show up for my family, my business, and myself in the best way possible.

THE SELF-DISCIPLINE BLUEPRINT

According to a 2020 *Forbes* article, "self-discipline is the bridge between goals defined and goals accomplished."[5] I couldn't have said it better myself. The article goes on to list nine powerful steps for cultivating self-discipline:

1. Know your strengths and weaknesses.
2. Remove temptations.
3. Set clear goals and have an execution plan.
4. Practise daily diligence.
5. Create new habits and rituals.
6. Change your perception about willpower.
7. Give yourself a backup plan.
8. Find trusted coaches or mentors.
9. Forgive yourself and move forward.

The blueprint is right there for anyone who's ready to cultivate and exercise the self-discipline needed to succeed in life. The best time to start is now.

There's no doubt about it – building a better life for you and your family requires discipline. What are your goals? What do you want to achieve in life? Write it all down, and make sure your objectives are clear. What's your action plan for making it happen? Once you have a plan in place, you can start working towards your intended outcome. Only through self-discipline and creating the right habits and routines will you be able to stay committed enough to see your plan through to completion. Once something becomes habitual, it requires much less thought and willpower and becomes easier to maintain. It's almost like you're running towards your goals on autopilot. At times, it can feel effortless. Once you start to build momentum, that's when it gets exciting. With momentum and growth comes more energy and drive to keep powering towards your goals. From there, results follow, and success flows.

I'm not saying the road won't occasionally, or even often, get rough and challenging, but, even in the tough times, you can keep moving forward, inching ever closer to the life you imagine. Don't beat yourself up if something doesn't go to plan. Just keep moving forward, and remember to celebrate the small wins, milestones, and achievements along the way.

Essentially, the key to living a good life is stability – and not just financial stability. I'm talking mental stability, physical stability, and, yes, financial stability. There's no point being financially free if you're working yourself to death to get there – like Steve Jobs – and you've ruined your relationships with your partner and kids. If your health deteriorates because you've been too focused on work to properly look after yourself, how good is all that money then? We should be looking at health and wealth holistically. You shouldn't need to sacrifice one for the other.

CAN MONEY BUY HAPPINESS?

Some people genuinely don't want or need a lot of money. Really, they just want a bit more control over their lives. They're happy to live minimalistic lifestyles as long as they can do it peacefully and spend time with the people they care about. In my online course, Financial Foundations, one of the first things I get people to do is think about and write down their vision. Although it's a course that focuses on financial freedom, I don't want them to focus *just* on the financial side of things. Instead, I ask them to state a vision for their personal lives, their businesses or careers, their relationships, and their health. These four areas are the pillars of the larger vision because they're all relevant to living a quality life. I've learnt the hard way that having one without the others leads to a life of emptiness, which I'll discuss more later.

Of course, you can't achieve perfect balance at all times, but it's a lot better than neglecting any one area completely. You could put all of your focus on your business or career, make a tidy fortune, and feel absolutely miserable because your relationships are in the shitter and you can't walk up a long flight of stairs without stopping to catch your breath. There are plenty of sour, miserable, rich people out there, and money's not the problem. Have you heard people say, "I'd rather be poor and happy?" Fuck that. Why would you say that? That's a poor person's mentality. No one's asking you to choose between happiness and wealth. Why can't you have it all? Well, you can. Sometimes we have to ask life for more than we think we deserve. You want to be poor and happy? Great. But what if you were well-off and happy? What could you achieve? You could be generous with your wealth, start a charity, help others, whatever meaningful act fulfils you. Money can't buy you authentic relationships or, in general, your health. It can, however, buy you the freedom of time to focus on these things and anything else that matters to you.

The big question is, can money buy happiness? A 2010 study found that happiness does increase with wealth but only up to a certain point. Once you reach above-average income and living standards – for example, an income of around US$75,000 per year at the time of the study – emotional wellbeing plateaus.[6] You don't get any happier.

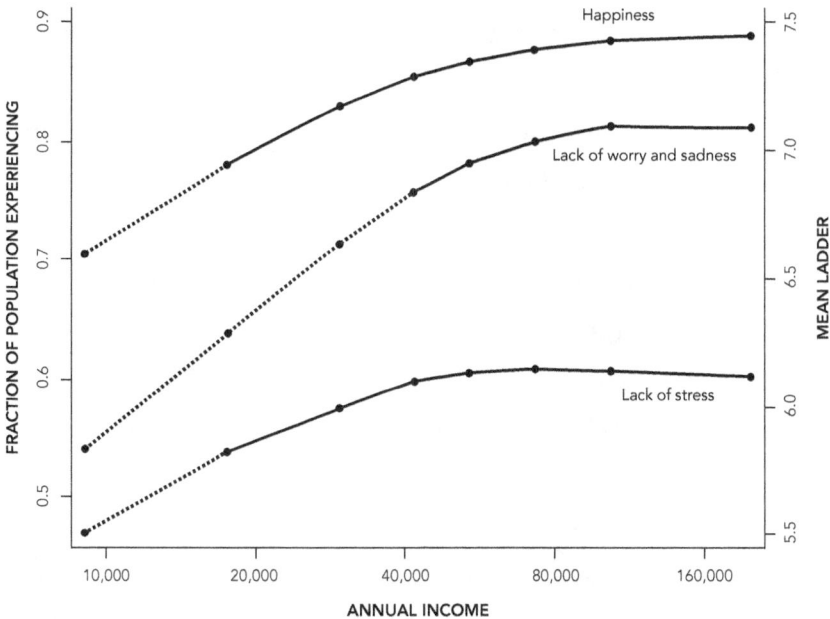

Relationship between income and different markers of happiness and wellbeing.

When we reduce stress, we have more energy and drive to find happiness and enjoy life. However, a high income doesn't always mean less stress. In fact, it could mean the opposite. If you're earning a lot of money but your job is very demanding and time-consuming, you'll likely experience more stress and have less free time to pursue your passions, unless, of course, your job *is* your passion.

With a realistic vision, achievable goals, and effective management of time and finances, you can potentially increase your wealth beyond the average income threshold and reach peak happiness. Of course, to truly experience peak happiness, you'll need to use your new financial position to create more free time and reduce stress in your life.

Essentially, most of us want to have enough money to live well and do the things we love with the people we love. If you're slaving away at a job, working insane hours, and constantly feeling under pressure, you might be doing more harm than good, working contradictory to the lifestyle you envision, even if you're maintaining your wealth. Don't get me wrong, achieving big things in life does require a lot of focus, time, and commitment. As you push towards your goals, you'll definitely experience moments of pressure and stress, but overcoming those challenging situations will bring you closer to realising your long-term vision. The key is to be mindful of those moments and try to restore balance when necessary.

I've seen so many entrepreneurs break themselves, getting completely run-down and burnt out, because they didn't achieve or maintain balance. In my mid-20s, I was guilty of this, running too hard too early, not realising it was a marathon, not a sprint. I wanted it all, and I wanted it now. When we fail to maintain balance, our mental and physical health can suffer, and, as we know, our health is our greatest asset.

So, what do *you* think is more important, health or wealth? Let me put it this way – a family friend of mine found out he was dying of cancer at 37 years old. It was really aggressive, and all the money in the world couldn't save him. The news hit me hard because here was a fairly young man, with six kids, who was on his way out. Dying of cancer at 37? At that age? I couldn't imagine not being here for my daughter. For me, the news was a cold dose of reality.

During an Easter long weekend, I was at a cafe, standing by our table, trying to rock my daughter to sleep in her carrier. A man got up from another table, shuffled over, and stopped near me. "Kane," he said. Who was this bloke? He looked about 65 years old. I must have been staring at him funny because he said his name. It was that same 37-year-old family friend – gaunt, frail, could barely walk, just beaten up from chemo. It broke my heart.

In his final days, what do you think he was thinking about? *What's the next big stock? Is it lithium? Should I invest in crypto? What if it pops and makes me 100 times return on investment? Is now a good time to buy my next investment property?* Fuck no! He didn't care about any of that stuff.

If you lose your wealth, it's not the end of the world. The money's still out there, and you can keep chasing it. But if you lose your health, well, once it's gone, it's gone.

LABELLED A 'YOUNG OFFENDER'

Before I got shipped off to Boys' Town, as I mentioned, I got put into the Young Offenders Act. Under the act, when juvenile delinquents, such as yours truly, get up to too much mischief, the state tries to rehabilitate them through the court system or programs run by the PCYC. They want to head kids off before they go too far down the wrong path, end up in jail, and become a burden on the system.

As we know, by consciously or subconsciously creating routines, certain behaviours can develop into habits, either good or bad. The programs created for young offenders aimed to prevent the formation of bad habits during youth to create more well-adjusted adults. Most of us can't completely control the behaviours we're exposed to; they're usually fixtures of our home and social environments, and, over time, other people's bad habits can creep in and become our own.

For example, have you ever finished dinner only to have some chocolate, ice cream, or another unhealthy snack suddenly appear in your hand? Do you ever question it? Where exactly did you get the habit of eating sweets after dinner? Is it a conscious or subconscious choice you're making? We all have many such habits whose origins we don't question. Over time, the things we're exposed to can influence our behaviours, create habits, and shape our routines. The trick is to *consciously* choose which habits we form, focusing on the good ones.

When I was put into the Young Offenders Act, Michelle Dury, the youth police officer running the program, was responsible for me from about age 13. Her focus was to get me into the gym and boxing as part of a regular routine. She encouraged me to stay active, letting me use the facilities and services for free. Of course, I had to be on my best behaviour, which I often was because I didn't want to get banned from the gym. It was positive reinforcement – and it worked. Not only did it encourage me to behave myself, but it also created a positive association with fitness. For us 'young offenders', exercise wasn't a punishment like it might be in a boot-camp-style situation. Instead, it was a reward.

At the PCYC, they sold pies on Tuesdays and Thursdays, and if I'd been behaving myself, Michelle would let me raid the pie warmer at the end of those days. So, at 13 years old, I'd bust myself in the gym to clear my head, and then I'd scoff down two or three pies, and maybe the odd finger bun or pastry – whatever was left. Hey, I was a growing boy, and, at that age, I had a pretty good metabolism, so I didn't notice the pies on the waistline. These days, it's a different story. One calorie too many, and the dad bod appears.

Michelle always checked the police record to see what I'd been up to, and if I'd been caught misbehaving – drinking, loitering, causing any mischief – I wouldn't be allowed in the gym.

"Don't let him in," Michelle would tell the staff.

"What? Why can't I use the gym?"

"The police report says you had an encounter with..."

"That's bullshit, Michelle." Yeah, I never took it well. Frequently, Michelle and I would argue like mother and son. That's the sort of relationship we had. She knew my mum quite well from all the meetings we'd had through the PCYC program, and she knew she wasn't well, so, with pies and gym access as rewards (or bribes), she went out of her way to try to steer me onto the right path.

Michelle also saved me from *really* fucking up a few times. One day, when I was home on suspension – back when I was still allowed at school – Mum had gone to work and left the car, so I decided to take it for a spin. I found the keys, hopped in the car, fired it up, and started reversing down the driveway. Before I made it out to the road, in the rear-view mirror, I saw a van pull up across the driveway behind me. On the side of the van were the letters 'PCYC'. It was Michelle.

She jumped out of the van and hurried towards the car, yelling, "What the hell are you doing?"

I was halfway out the driveway, keys in the ignition, engine still running. So, yeah, I didn't have a great excuse for that one. Thankfully, Michelle decided to come and check on me while I was suspended; otherwise, I would have got onto the road and done who knows what. I could have crashed the car. I could have injured someone. I could have created another big problem for myself and Mum that neither of us needed. Was the car even insured? I doubt it. We were still struggling financially, and it's unlikely that paying a hefty insurance premium was at the top of Mum's priorities. Thankfully, Michelle showed up in the right place at the right time. Looking back, her arrival was a blessing.

During that time, Michelle was a positive force in my life. She did that job for 30 years, creating multiple programs and helping countless young people find a better path. We lost contact for a while, but we've since reconnected, and I consider her a friend. She's a great lady and a genuine role model in my life and in the lives of many others. I can't thank Michelle enough for her work and everything she has done over the years.

Later, I became the poster boy for the PCYC programs, talking to kids at high schools, presenting on different topics, and sharing my story and turning points with teenagers on similar paths to mine. Can you imagine? I certainly wouldn't have believed it at the time, back when I was in the Young Offenders program, arguing with Michelle about gym privileges and free pies. But hey, if someone like me can turn it all around, anyone can. The story doesn't end there, though. There were plenty more fuckups in my future before I stepped onto the right path. In fact, my situation got a whole lot worse before it got better.

BIGGEST INSIGHTS FROM THE FIRST CHAPTER OF MY LIFE

Budgeting – A budget is the oxygen of your financial world, giving you the ability to manage, control, and structure your money. Always have a budget. If you don't have one, sit down and take control of your money now. It doesn't matter how much you earn – if you can't control your spending and don't have the ability to put money aside to invest, save, and spend wisely on your future, you'll struggle to attain financial freedom.

Different avenues to success – Don't beat yourself up if you don't finish school as number one or get the top score on a test. Remember, there are a lot of avenues to success, and there are strengths you have or could develop that will help you in life. School is only the first big test on your journey and takes up, on average, only 22 percent of your life (based on living to the standard life expectancy age).

Health and wellness – Remember to look after your health while you build your wealth. Burnout is real, and stress is a big killer – it will reduce your life span. Even if you have all the money in the world, you can't buy back good health, so make sure you continue to learn, and invest a good, balanced portion of your time and money in protecting your greatest asset.

Creating a vision – Sit down and set a clear vision. Break down your goals for your finances and how much money you need to create the life you want, and, in this process, think about what will truly make you happy, aside from the money, as this won't be enough. Remember, success isn't defined by dollars in your bank account. It's about creating a lifestyle that's true and meaningful to you, and you alone, or your family – no one else, and no one else's family. Hence why you need a vision, a target, some clear goals, and steps to get more than your finances right. With balance between your career, business, health, and personal achievements in front of mind, a holistic vision will help you improve your happiness and overall wellbeing.

Focus on the future – Don't let your past and your mistakes dictate who you are today and who you can become or show up as in the future. The past helps you become the person you need to be. Remember, when you start to focus on doing good things, being good, and becoming a better version of yourself, other people will show up to help you get there. In my experience, it's like an unwritten law of the universe, and it has worked for me. The more you follow your true calling and live authentically, the more the doors of opportunity open. I'm not saying they are all easy doors to walk through, but they do present themselves, and the more you lean into this way of living, the better life becomes.

KANE AT PCYC PROGRAM

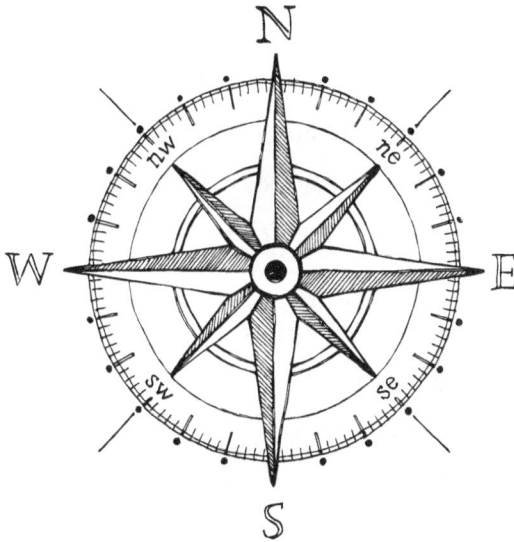

CHAPTER 2

DESCENT INTO
THE UNDERWORLD

A PLACE FOR NAUGHTY KIDS

Going into Boys' Town – now called Dunlea Centre because it now also helps young girls, not just boys – was daunting. Firstly, I was going into a new, unknown environment. Secondly, I was surrounded by other naughty kids, living with them full-time. On top of all that, I had to adapt to curfews, being told when to study, when to eat, when to go to bed. We lost a lot of the control we had over our lives, adhering to a strict structure that ruled our days.

The thing is, most kids *need* structure. Even if they don't outwardly say it, subconsciously, they practically thirst for it. At Boys' Town, naturally, there was a bit of resistance, from me and others, to the enforced routine and structure, but eventually we all fell into sync and accepted the new social norm. Most of us, anyway. There's always bound to be an outlier or two.

Boys' Town wasn't a radical boot camp situation – far from it. We still had access to pool and ping-pong tables, outdoor sports, an old PlayStation, and other recreational activities. The centre operated on a behaviour reward system. It was simple: if you were well-behaved, you got access to all the fun stuff; if you were naughty, you lost those privileges. Thanks to Michelle at the PCYC, I had experience with this type of reward system, so I fell into it naturally. Many of the kids, including myself, didn't have ping-pong tables or anything like that at home, so the rewards were pretty effective.

Of course, some kids struggled with being told 'no'. But what could they do? Their parents weren't there to cave in and give them what they wanted, so they had no choice but to accept the new situation they were in.

The system has since evolved into one where if you misbehave, you can still redeem yourself and earn back your privileges. They actually make it quicker and easier to earn redemption than punishment because they want to train good behaviour. If you're training a dog, you wouldn't – or shouldn't – smack it for not performing the right action. Instead, you reward it when it *does* do the right thing, reinforcing that behaviour. Obviously, humans aren't dogs, but we share more similarities than you might think. At Boys' Town, the approach got results, and most of us turned into fairly disciplined little humans.

We also built good habits around basic household tasks and chores. Every week, we would wash our sheets, a great habit to get into. It's something that most teenage boys – and many adults – don't do. They're in their rooms making a mess, with porno magazines and whatever else, so it can get quite unhygienic. We also rotated cooking duties, which meant, every week, a couple of boys would be responsible for planning the menu, buying ingredients, and cooking the meals. At the most basic level, we all brushed our teeth two times a day, showered, and made our beds in the mornings.

Look, it wasn't all fun, games, and structure for everyone. As I'm sure you can imagine, some really rough kids ended up at Boys' Town, some really interesting characters. On my first day there, one kid, Henry, rocked up on the Monday morning in a stolen car. He just parked it in the car park and strolled in like everything was fine.

For most of us, the system had taught us to stop believing in ourselves. We were conditioned to think we were the naughty kids, so we played out that belief. What happens when you lock up a bunch of naughty kids together? They be naughty together. It could be chaos at times. Fights would break out; chairs would get thrown; kids would get smashed in the face with pool cues – everything you can imagine. When you've got some of the naughtiest kids in Sydney all locked up in one place, kids who were too rebellious for the school system, you're going to get some wild moments. Boys would lash out, but the staff were quick to punish them and pull them back into line.

Many of the kids came from toxic home environments, where lashing out, screaming, and verbal abuse were common, so adjusting to the new social norm didn't happen overnight, but, deep down, I think most of us appreciated the structure. Even something as simple as sitting down to dinner at the same time every night was a welcome change for many of us.

At Boys' Town, they let us smoke cigarettes, but only at certain times of the day and not in our rooms. It was a matter of choosing which battles to fight and which weren't worth the struggle. Yes, smoking is terrible for your health, and they could have banned it outright, but then they would've had kids sneaking cigarettes into the centre and smoking in their rooms. For kids in our situation, smoking was the least of our troubles, so they just let us have that one. There were bigger battles to fight. Mainly, the focus was on academics and, of course, decency, which mostly meant being polite and not smashing each other in the face with pool cues.

When I left Boys' Town a year after arriving, I took many of the habits I built there with me. I still make my bed every morning; I still wash my sheets once a week, and I still eat a good, hearty dinner every night. Everything I do now is quite structured, and I've no doubt got Boys' Town to thank. I definitely built some good habits there, and good habits can set you up for a lifetime of success. You won't get far without forming at least a few. Unfortunately, even with some good habits under my belt, success was still a long way off.

ARE YOU READY FOR AN UNCOMFORTABLE TRUTH?

At Boys' Town, I learnt the value of structure and discipline. It was forced structure and discipline, but the behaviour stuck with me, nonetheless. Now, I'm not saying everyone needs to be locked up with a bunch of juvenile delinquents to get their shit together – not at all. Structure is something *you* can introduce into your life, and discipline is something you can build over time. Don't think you'll develop monk-level discipline overnight. Most of us don't adapt that easily. So, how *do* you build discipline? One deliberate action at a time.

Psychologist Jordan Peterson might be the most famous proponent of the 'make your bed' philosophy. If you're struggling to find structure or build discipline, you've got to start with something small. So, make your bed. Do it first thing in the morning and see what happens from there. Even if the rest of the day is a chaotic mess, at least you accomplished *something*. At least you exercised some level of discipline. It's an early win, which sets the tone for the rest of the day.

Once you're consistently doing the small tasks, like making your bed in the morning, you can move on to bigger goals, like exercising every day. Frankly, you're probably not quite ready to take on the world when your life, your house, your room is a mess. The problem is, most people *aren't* fixing their own problems before they try to fix other people's. For instance, they might be ranting about the government misspending taxpayers' money while their own finances are in a shambles.

Whether you want to develop discipline or build wealth, you need to start with small steps and incrementally move towards the larger goal. For example, you wouldn't start with the immediate goal of making $1 million this year if you're currently making $40K. Instead, you might start with a lower number *and* create a plan to get there and beyond. If you set a big goal, you better have a big heart and the work ethic to back it up. Eventually, you might make that first million, but it will be the incremental steps that get you there, not one giant leap. Don't expect a winning lottery ticket to save the day. There are no shortcuts to success or great results. You've got to do the work.

If you want to become a millionaire from nothing, you're going to need a good job. I see a lot of young people coming out of university, expecting a top-end job and career right out of the gate. Can you imagine their surprise when they realise the world doesn't work like that? For most of us, to get to the top, we have to eat shit at the bottom first – and I've eaten my fair share, which I'll get to later. If you're not willing to do the difficult, dirty, unglamorous jobs, you're probably not cut out for the big league.

With anything, you need to be realistic with your expectations. To go big, you must first start small. Develop good habits. Learn good behaviours. Build discipline over time. These are the small actions that will gradually help you develop specific skills for success in any area of life. How was the Great Wall of China built? One brick at a time. If you tried to tell someone they had to build something like that, a 20,000 km wall, they'd feel overwhelmed.

Man, do you know how many bricks would go into a 20,000 km wall? They'd lose hope. But the Great Wall of China *did* get built. It just took 2000 years or so. Don't expect overnight success. It almost never happens.

Even when you do achieve success, you'll need that discipline more than ever. People see my success and think it's all fun and games from here on in – but it's not. My job is actually quite repetitive. My day-to-day activities are very similar and follow the same processes and structures. My conversations are almost all the same. My days are all the same: review the books, train staff, go over reports, check and produce numbers or strategies for clients. It's not like we're taking a cookie-cutter approach, but the phone calls, the video calls, the client meetings, the paperwork are often the same, or at least it feels that way after more than a decade doing it. To deal with the monotony of doing the same thing over and over again, day in, day out, and stay focused on the end goal, I have to be disciplined. Those boring, repetitive tasks are what build the most success and wealth for the business. I may not enjoy every part of the process, but I've built enough discipline over the years that it doesn't bother me. I simply do what needs to be done.

Getting in shape is the same. If you want to lose weight, build muscle, whatever, you don't just go to the gym for half an hour then walk out looking jacked, or with a sixpack. It doesn't work that way. To get serious results, you need to work out regularly, watch what you eat, recover properly, and, importantly, be consistent. Doing one big, 10-hour workout every two weeks won't cut it. It's the 1-hour workout five days a week over an extended period of time that will be most effective. It's a lengthy process that involves many incremental steps and a whole lot of discipline.

Frequently, I get people who come to me and say, "I want to make heaps of money." They want to get rich, and they want it quick. Often, they're eyeing off things like crypto and other high-risk ventures. I have to explain to them that making money is a slow, monotonous, often boring process. It's not sexy at all. You've got to be disciplined and consistent. You work, get paid, put money aside, work, get paid, put money aside, and repeat until you've reached your goal, all the while watching your budget and making good investments. Boring, right? It is, but it's also necessary. If a potential client can't understand that, I'm not the guy to help them, and I send them on their way.

In business, if you don't have discipline, you'll struggle to deal with the bad days, the days where you want to quit, walk away, burn it all to the ground. Those days *will* come, and white-knuckling your way through them, relying on willpower alone, won't cut it. Willpower is a limited resource and when you run out due to excess pressure or a heavy workload, you need something to fall back on. With a clear vision, combined with discipline, structure, routines, and rituals, you can push through even the toughest challenges and come out the other side intact, ready to face the next obstacle. When you build the right behaviours for success, over time, they become habitual, automated. You don't have to force them anymore. They're a part of your lifestyle, a part of who you are or who you've become in the process.

So many people want the instant fix or the get-rich-quick scheme. I've worked with marketers who tell me, to get attention, I need to sell the big-ticket item that promises the world, but I'm not that guy. It's not what we do. It's not realistic. They argue that's what I'm competing with online; it's what my competitors are offering. So what? I don't want to be like them, out there flogging bullshit, but that's what salespeople like to do, and that just isn't me.

"Get shredded in two weeks…"

"Become a millionaire in six months with this one strategy the rich don't want you to know…"

"Here are the five proven steps to ultimate success…"

It's all overhyped nonsense. As someone who has dragged himself from the bottom to the top, I can assure you there's no secret recipe for success. Don't get me wrong, there are definitely things that will significantly improve your chances of getting results, but the main thing is you've got to be prepared to work for them. If you bite it off, you better be ready to chew and swallow. The grind isn't easy, but staying where you are now might not be easy either, especially when you start looking back with regret at what you could have done to change your situation. You could either choose continued suffering, resigning to your current lifestyle, or you could start pushing towards a better future, one step at a time. Both options involve pain and struggle, but one has the potential for a happy ending. Would you rather climb the mountain with a good chance of reaching the top? Or would you rather sit at the bottom, complaining about the view? Do you want to experience the sacrifice and struggle of pushing towards a goal? Or would you prefer the pain and suffering of regret, knowing you could have done something but didn't even try? The choice is yours.

"We must all suffer from one of two pains: the pain of discipline or the pain of regret. The difference is discipline weighs ounces while regret weighs tons."

– JIM ROHN

UNDER THE (POSITIVE) INFLUENCE

Gerard was one of the counsellors at Boys' Town. He was a surfy guy, around 30 years old, played in a band, and was an absolute legend. He would often sit with us, talk to us, and try to understand what would motivate us to improve our lives.

He had a tough gig, trying to get into the minds of stubborn teenage boys. Due to trauma, violence, and abuse, many of us put up high walls and were very resistant to being open. On the exterior, we were tough kids who didn't give a fuck about anything, but, on the inside, we were scared, broken children who didn't know how to express ourselves. We were either one conversation away from breaking down and crying or, worse, not being able to share to the point that we believed the easier way out was to take our own lives.

However, Gerard would always try to get us to open up and question the paths we were on. Often, it was simply a matter of finding the right angle.

"Oh, so you're this tough guy then?" Gerard asked one day.

"No, I don't know."

"So, you're *not* a tough guy?"

"I suppose I am then," I replied, annoyed at his counter response.

"You got a little sister?"

"Yeah... Why?"

"What type of guy would you like her to date when she grows up?"

What sort of question is that? I thought about it and, after several seconds of silence, responded. "A good guy that was nice to her."

"Okay, great. What do you think a good guy looks and acts like?"

"I don't know."

He probed further and got me thinking about all the traits of a 'good guy' and who I'd want dating my sister. When someone takes you down that line of thought, you can't just say, "I don't give a shit," not when it's about your sister, or mother, or daughter, whoever it might be. Of course you want them to date a good guy. Gerard's words dug deep.

"Now think about the type of girl you want to date," he said. "What would she be like?"

I described my dream girl like any teenage boy would: smart, nice, caring, borderline supermodel looks...

"Okay, great. And if she had a brother, or maybe her father, what would you want him to think of you?"

I didn't want to say I'd want him to think I was a good guy. I was too tough, too stubborn. *Why would I give a fuck what some girl's brother or father thinks?*

He continued. "If you met this girl's brother or father for the first time, do you think he'd be happy with who she's dating? Do you think he'd be okay with the fact that you don't have a job?

You smoke? You're here at Boys' Town? What would he think? Wouldn't he want the best for her? What about her mother, her other family members, and friends? Imagine you've met this amazing girl, she's everything you ever wanted. What would you want the people in her life to think of you? Do you think they'd accept you? You can change, of course. But do you think they'd accept you as you are now?"

"I..." *Fuck this guy. He's messing with my head.*

But he had a point. It just took some time for it to sink in and settle before I could accept that Gerard was right. *If I met a really nice girl, wouldn't I want her to think I was a good guy? Wouldn't I want to have a good job? Wouldn't I want her to think I had my head screwed on right? What would she think if she saw me hanging out in the streets, smoking, with my ripped FUBU jeans? Would she think I was cool? Honestly, she'd think I was a bit of a grub, and her family – there's no way they'd accept me.* At this point, I was already considered an outsider by most of society. I mean, my own family would have disowned me if we weren't the same blood.

Gerard planted the seed that got me thinking about the type of person I wanted to be – and I'm not talking about who I wanted to be professionally or financially. He got me thinking about my values and how I wanted to live. *What do I really want out of life? Who do I want to become? What do I want people to think of me or feel when they encounter me in life?*

"I want a better future for myself and my family," I said. "I want better than what I had growing up." Beyond a good girlfriend, I was now talking about family and the long-term future.

"Okay," he said, "that's great. So, right now, what are you going to do to make that happen?"

At that point, I hit a mental block. I didn't have an answer. What *was* I going to do to make that happen? I didn't know, but I knew I wanted to be someone better than who I was right then. But how would I get there?

When I had no real role models in my life – I had no father figure, let alone my actual father – I used to look up to Dwayne 'The Rock' Johnson. Here's a tough-looking guy, who has faced many adversities, working his way up from the bottom, yet he has such a calm nature. People love him but if he wanted to, he could rip your head off. He's *huge*, but he's a gentle giant. He's also a great dad, has a strong presence, and is highly disciplined. In his life, he has faced challenges, but he has made all the right decisions. He hasn't needed to bend the rules or do wrong by people. He just does what needs to be done – that is, he keeps working hard and does things the *right* way.

"Not only do I think being nice and kind is easy,
but being kind, in my opinion, is important."
– DWAYNE 'THE ROCK' JOHNSON

The Rock was definitely a big influence in my life. To me, he was an influencer before the term became commonplace. The label makes sense though. If both parents are working flat out, kids *will* turn to their friends, and now even the internet, for support, and the people they find there *will* influence their lives, for better or worse.

Thankfully, my celebrity role model was Dwayne 'The Rock' Johnson. It could have been a lot worse.

LEARNING THE HOUSING COMMISSION WAY OF LIFE

While I was at Boys' Town, my younger sister took my room. So, when I finally came home, at 16 years old, I had nowhere to sleep. For a while, I slept on a mattress on the living room floor, but I couldn't just live there with my shit all over the place, so when I met a girl who lived in a block of housing commission units, I moved in with her and her parents. There were four of us in a small two-bedroom unit. I didn't realise it at the time, but it was a really disturbing environment, with kids running amuck and drug-addicted parents not noticing or caring. I'm not saying everyone in housing commission is a negligent addict – they're not – but I saw a lot of heartbreaking situations when I was there.

The block of units was U-shaped, with a grassy area in the centre, where kids of all ages – 3, 4, 5 years old and upwards – would play until 10 pm or later in the middle of winter, wearing nothing but dirty, ripped shorts and T-shirts. Sometimes, no one came to call the kids home, so I'd go looking for their parents. There were probably 100 or so units in the complex, but I'd got to know most of the residents, so I knew which kids belonged where. When taking a kid home, it wasn't uncommon to find their unit door unlocked, sometimes not even closed, and their parents smacked out on methadone, passed out on the lounge. The curtains would be closed, the house dark, with graffiti all over the walls.

Surprisingly, however, some of the people I met had great

values. While they had no money, they were still better role models than a lot of the rich people I've met. Sometimes, the people who are supposed to be the most upstanding citizens have the least regard for other humans, whereas some of the most povo housing commission residents have the most admirable morals and loyalty in their hearts.

For example, my then-girlfriend's mum, Sally, was as poor as they came, drank a lot, and was dealing with an extreme domestic violence situation, but, at the same time, she had a big heart. Often, when she only had a meagre $5 left from her last Centrelink payment, she'd go and buy a big box of Weet-Bix and a carton of milk, bring all the kids in, and feed them. There was no milk in the fridge until she bought it, and she didn't have a microwave – yep, to some people, a microwave is a luxury – so she'd boil water in the kettle to heat up the Weet-Bix for the kids. Thanks to Sally, many hungry kids went to bed with food in their bellies. To look at her, you might have thought she was a social degenerate, a no-hoper, but, on the inside, she was a kind-hearted lady with exceptional values. As she used to say, she'd give the shirt off her own back to help someone.

One day, at a train station in Sydney, after witnessing a moment I'd never forget, I came to an important realisation. I was with my girlfriend and her mum, and a weathered, old lady was trying to get up the stairs with a big suitcase and a trolley. It was peak hour, and people were pushing past her to get to wherever they were going. I'm talking people in designer suits, with perfect haircuts, wearing expensive watches – *successful* people. But no one stopped to help her. They were meant to be the cream of society's crop, the *winners*, yet they didn't give a shit about that struggling, old lady. They didn't even blink as they elbowed their way past her while she fought her way up the stairs. The rush-hour stampede of corporates pushed their way through because they, of course, were more important. They had places to be! Were these good people? I'm not saying they were *bad* people but when Sally noticed the lady struggling, she rushed to help. To me, that was the reaction of a good person. Right there, she demonstrated more heart and compassion than any of the successful go-getters at the train station. In their defence, having busy lives and being stressed with unmanageable time-lines and workloads can cause people to lose their awareness. They become unaware of the simple deeds we can do for others in need. Sally taught me to always try to help people when you can – an important lesson I held on to for the rest of my life.

As I considered the contrasting values of Sally, who'd give her last dollar to feed a hungry kid, and the corporate suits at the station, who'd push past a struggling, old lady, I realised you don't need to be financially successful to have good morals. You can be a good person, no matter where you stand in life, whether you're living in a cramped housing commission unit in a rough neighbourhood or a spacious mansion by the beach. This is why knowing who you want to become in the pursuit of your vision is important, as money can, and often does, change people. Knowing the type of human you want to be is crucial. If you find yourself straying from that ideal, you can make corrections where needed, always staying true to yourself. Don't worry, it took me some time to get it all together, but I always stayed true to who I wanted to be, the person I felt I was deep down.

During this time, I was starting to solidify my values, and I knew one thing for certain: if I ever pulled myself out of the hole I was in and became successful, I wouldn't be the soulless man in a suit, who ignored the struggles of others. Instead, I'd be more like Sally, offering a helping hand – or a bowl of Weet-Bix – to those in need.

THAT'S A FACT

When it comes to developing our values, studies show that students without clear values are less likely to succeed and more likely to pick up bad habits, make poor decisions, and gravitate towards alcohol, drugs, and crime.[7]

Developing your vision, with goals and a plan, is important, but so is supporting that vision with solid values. If you're unsure about your values, look to people in your life – or outside of it – who you'd like to emulate. For me, it was Dwayne 'The Rock' Johnson. I wasn't necessarily chasing his level of success, and I definitely didn't want to be a WWE wrestler, but his values and work ethic resonated with me. He was the role model I needed to avoid losing myself in the world. If you're struggling with your values, find your own Rock to guide you.

A SERIES OF SHITTY JOBS

Because money was tight, I couldn't finish year 12, so I decided to – or Mum decided I should – get a trade. I was good at maths, so I ended up getting a job as an apprentice electrician.

As an apprentice, I was maybe earning a couple of hundred bucks a week. It doesn't exactly inspire someone to stay on the straight and narrow now, does it? By then, I owed around $20,000 in fines for fare dodging at the train station, underage smoking, being disobedient with police, and a few other things from the past. Because I owed so much money, I couldn't get my licence, which is another example of the system holding people back, holding them down. With no qualifications and no licence, how was I meant to compete with other kids who hadn't fucked up when they were younger and accumulated a pile of unpaid fines?

While I was fortunate to get the electrician gig, not having a licence meant I had to carry my toolbox, along with a backpack full of food and other bits and pieces, up a steep hill to the train station at 4:30 am every day. If it was raining, well, then I also had to carry an umbrella if I didn't want to be soaking wet when I got to the station. Once I got onsite, the day usually consisted of constantly being barked at and told what to do. At knock-off time, I'd get home the same way, stinking up the train because I'd been sweating all day while doing low-end jobs. Was *this* life as a working adult? I felt underpaid, underappreciated, and underwhelmed with the situation I was in.

The thing is, I could've put in the effort, embraced the grind, and made a career in the industry. It's not like you can't make decent money as a tradie if you play it smart. The truth is, I never put in the effort with that job. I wasn't willing to take the small steps needed to reach a bigger goal. At that point, my past decisions were the exact reflection of my reality, meaning my choices, no one else's, had made my life harder.

I ended up losing my electrician job. Because I hated it so much, I called in sick a lot, and you can only take so many unexplained sick days before they cut you loose. I couldn't handle all the monotonous, labour-intensive work. I wanted to cut to the chase and do the fun stuff, like wiring things up, but I wasn't willing to spend time and effort gaining the skills, experience, and knowledge I needed. I suppose it was the fact that I didn't want it bad enough. The job was Mum's idea; she thought it would be good for me. Whether I really wanted it or not, I didn't want to *work* for it. Unfortunately for me, working hard is one of the main drivers of success. With my attitude, the job was never going to last. I was never going to apply myself because it wasn't a career I'd chosen to pursue, and I wasn't motivated to try.

Next, I got a job at a tyre wholesale business, stacking tyres onto trucks in a warehouse. It was more monotonous work, so, naturally, I didn't last long. I do, however, remember something about the job that stuck with me.

In the warehouse, there was a small office with a flat roof, with a toilet and a kitchenette inside. The memorable thing about this office was the desk and chair that always sat on the roof, which you could access via a set of stairs around the back. Occasionally, the owner of the business would sit up there with his laptop, smoking cigars, and looking out over his little tyre empire.

Who is this guy? He rocks up in his fancy car whenever he wants and barely does anything. He just sits up there, puffing a cigar. The top dog!

He never really said much to anyone besides the general manager, just checked on things, smoked a few cigars, then pissed off in his nice car.

How did he do it? Whenever I saw someone successful, I'd always ask myself that question: How did they do it? I was never jealous that they were making money – nothing like that – I genuinely wanted to know how they did it. *What did they do? How did they become so successful? Was it timing? Was it resilience? Was it dumb luck? Was it something they inherited or were given somehow?* No matter what, I'd always ask myself the question… *How did they do it?*

When you study successful people, you can determine what they're doing right and what you're doing wrong. However, I do have a word of warning: trying to mimic someone else's path to success may not take you to the same place. Sometimes, yes, it can be beneficial. Other times, however, it can be detrimental. For example, you could be trying to copy a decade-old strategy that might not work in today's environment. The world changes, and you need to cherrypick the knowledge that's relevant *now*. I do, however, strongly believe that success leaves clues and if you want to find them, you need to look closely at what successful people have done to get to where they are. You'll soon start to recognise similar patterns and traits.

THAT'S A FACT

For many years, no one could break the four-minute mile. "It's impossible," people said. "Your heart would explode!" They came up with a lot of crazy excuses for why it couldn't be done.

In short, English neurologist Roger Bannister decided it *could* be done. How did he prove it? By doing it. In 1954, Roger ran the first sub-four-minute mile in recorded history.[8] But it wasn't all about physical training; it was also about mental discipline and belief.

The craziest thing about this story... In a little over a month, an Australian runner also broke the four-minute mile barrier, followed by many more in the years to come. It goes to show the power of mindset and belief in achieving our goals. As Norman Vincent Peale says, "Shoot for the moon. Even if you miss, you'll land among the stars."

After I left the tyre wholesaler, I got a job at Pickles Auctions, which sells off a lot of ex-government and ex-corporate fleets, along with repossessed vehicles. I worked in the car wash, so I got to drive a lot of the cars on the auction floor. Eventually, I moved up to prestige vehicles, where I got to drive Ferraris, Lamborghinis, Bentleys, and Rolls-Royces.

The experience was a bit of an eye-opener. On auction days, people would show up loaded with money. It wasn't unusual to see someone casually drop $400K on a car. Once, I watched an auction for number plates, and some were going for six figures. *Who are these people? Where did they get all that money?* Here I was, earning $500 a week washing cars, heavily in debt to the state government, with no licence, and these people could stroll in and drop half a mil on a second-hand Bentley like it was nothing.

I'd never be able to buy a nice car if I spent all my time washing them, so I left the auction house and returned to electrical work to try to finish what I'd started. To me, it seemed like a better path to achieving something in my life. So, off I went, getting a job with an air conditioning company owned by a guy named Turkish Mick.

TWO VERY DIFFERENT ROADS TO SUCCESS

Turkish Mick was a big, muscly bloke, late 30s, clean-cut, always well-dressed. Oh, and he was best friends with prominent King's Cross figure John Ibrahim. I read John's book many years later and learnt more about the relationship. They eventually, let's say, went different ways and weren't on good terms when Mick left. Mick's company did the electrical work and serviced the air conditioners in John's many nightclubs, his house, and also the massive houses of friends in their circle, always in prestigious areas. Once again, my low-paying job was about to give me a preview of what success could look like.

Before I knew it, I was in John's house by the water in Dover Heights, looking out over the Pacific Ocean, where I witnessed a whole new world. Suddenly, I was surrounded by wealth and success. John had model girlfriends, nice cars – Ferraris, Range Rovers – and rows of flashing pokie machines in the house. I couldn't believe what I was seeing. *What did this guy do to be able to live like this?* At the time, I was just a teenager, only 18 years old, who'd rocked up to do some electrical work, but I got a glimpse of what life could look like if I took a, let's say, unconventional path. To me, it looked pretty fucking good at first sight.

Many of the boys who I met at Boys' Town and on the streets were starting to pursue that sort of lifestyle, selling drugs and finding other unconventional ways to earn a living. When you're young and dumb and see people at the top living the good life, it looks really cool on the outside, but you don't understand the risks involved until you're in it. By then, it might be too late.

In John, I saw a path to wealth and success. I knew it wasn't the only option, but, compared to others, it felt more within my grasp, with my high school expulsion, résumé filled with low-paying, unskilled jobs, and Boys' Town as my last attended school.

During family Christmas gatherings, I'd often chat to my uncle, Keith. When he met my mum's sister at university, he was just an average guy. I mean, he wasn't particularly wealthy or successful. However, he eventually became a big-time corporate guy in the banks, retiring in his 50s in a nice house by the water. Uncle Keith had taken a straighter, much less contentious path to success than John. He studied hard, earned three degrees, and worked his arse off to get to the top of the corporate ladder. It was a grind, but it was a fairly safe ascent. When you work at a bank, your colleagues aren't likely to stab you if you piss them off. Unlike some, Uncle Keith lived to enjoy the fruits of his labour.

But I wasn't an academic. I wasn't capable of earning three degrees. I wasn't even capable of finishing high school. On one hand, I had John's example of success. On the other hand, I had Uncle Keith's. Which one was more achievable? I already had one foot in the underworld. I knew a lot of the people; I under-stood how that world worked, and I didn't need a fancy degree to start earning money. After being so beaten down by life, that was my mindset. That's all I thought I was capable of – a life of crime, basically. It didn't help that my job sucked.

As we know, at school, I was always the kid who constantly got into trouble. I never felt like I could be proud of my achievements, and I believed I'd never amount to anything, especially when I was living in housing commission and experiencing the low end of the living standards scale. I thought that was where I belonged. I never thought I'd have a good job, so I never considered working towards one. Clearly, my self-worth was at a rock-bottom low. It wasn't that long ago that I was a young kid, playing up in school, fighting for what I thought was right, standing up for the weak, and refusing to be a follower. I didn't want to be an employee, slaving away for years on end to maybe live an okay life. I wanted to make a better life for me and my family right now. Essentially, I wanted the quick fix, and the unconventional path looked more appealing every day.

I've always had trouble working for other people, being told what to do. I've always struggled doing what's expected or normal, especially in school. The sit down, shut up, blend in, fall in line, do your homework model didn't resonate with me. It just made me restless for something more. Now I realise I had an entrepreneurial mindset, but I didn't understand that then, and I didn't know where to direct that energy.

When I worked those shitty jobs and saw others' success, I didn't have an open line of communication with the people I was observing. The guy who owned the tyre warehouse was too high up on his throne, with his endless supply of cigars. The people who came onto the auction floor and dropped hundreds of thousands of dollars on luxury cars weren't going to give me the time of day. Why would they? Uncle Keith was always happy to chat, but I'd already examined his path, and I knew it wasn't for me. So, where did that leave me?

As I got closer with people who were operating on the fringes of society, a new path began to open up to me. It was sexy, exciting, and, importantly, *lucrative*. When I looked into the underworld, I saw money everywhere. I knew the streets; I had connections, and no one gave a shit that I didn't finish high school or have a degree. I knew I wasn't going to be a doctor, or a lawyer, or an engineer, but, at the same time, I knew I could be *something*.

So, I took the leap and decided to go all in on the one thing I thought I could do.

THE CROSSROAD MOMENT

Do you want to know the truth about the underworld? It's not so pretty on the inside. On the surface, you see all the glamour: the money and the cars and the big houses and the model girlfriends. But reality doesn't match what's advertised.

Behind the scenes, the majority of people aren't the John Ibrahims of the world. They aren't living in beachside mansions, and they aren't driving $600K Bentleys. I'm not saying they aren't making money, but there's a food chain, and most people aren't, and never will be, at the top. Some don't make it out alive. Many end up in jail, separated from their kids, their partners, their friends, their families for years on end. Basically, they end up ruining their lives.

Like me, they step into the world with one idea how things will be only to have it backfire in a big way. It's very rare that someone makes it through without getting shot, killed, or put in jail.

The brotherhood they talk about… it's all bullshit. There's constant betrayal, backstabbing, and snitching. Everyone's on edge. There's a lot of paranoia – and for good reason. They're constantly living in fear, looking over their shoulders, wondering when their time will come. For most people, it's not a glamorous life. It's a constant struggle to stay one step ahead of everyone around you.

You're going to face adversities in life. You're going to struggle, no matter what you do. The thing is, you can pick your adversities. You can pick your struggles. At that point in my life, I *could* have chosen to continue my electrical apprenticeship, build my skill set, and eventually start my own business, but it wasn't a struggle I was willing to accept. Instead, I chose a life of fear and uncertainty. I wanted the easy money, but, as I learnt, there's no such thing. Eventually, you start to hear things. You start to see things. You start to realise it's only a matter of time before you become another casualty of 'the good life'.

Gradually, the glamour did fade, and I saw the ugly reality. Was I willing to continue risking my own safety for money? Was I willing to keep living in fear? Was I willing to put my own family at risk? Soon after becoming associated with that world and the people in it, I seriously started to question the decision I'd made.

At around this time, when I was 19, Mum bought the book *Rich Dad Poor Dad* by Robert T Kiyosaki. She knew I was a bit different, always coming up with crazy ideas, so she thought the book might help me find my path. She was good like that, always trying to steer me back on track. No matter how far I wandered, she was always in the distance, doing what she could. In the book, Poor Dad, who has plenty of qualifications and what he believes to be job security, loses his job due to a recession. Rich Dad, on the other hand, is an entrepreneur and investor and has set himself up financially to weather the storm, with a range of skills and income streams. He cracked the wealth code, and I began to believe I could too. Becoming successful took him time and hard work, which was something I needed to hear. I needed that dose of reality. Through *Rich Dad Poor Dad*, I began to see other paths, other opportunities. Maybe I didn't need to die in the streets or end up in jail after all. Maybe I didn't need three degrees, impressive academic accolades, and all the other achievements I believed were out of reach. Maybe there was yet another way to create financial freedom and a better life.

Gradually, I pulled away from the underworld and, at age 20, got a job as a second-hand car salesman (don't judge me). I was still struggling with my finances, and the path of easy money kept calling me back. Resisting the urge to give in and go back to what I knew was difficult.

While selling cars, I met Patrick, who was the son of a very successful property developer. Patrick, who was in his late 30s, understood all the topics from *Rich Dad Poor Dad*: shares, property investment, taxation – all of it. Patrick had also read the book and, importantly, put it all into practice. For the next six months, Patrick and I spoke daily about the ins and outs of investing. With him, I was in a real-life mentoring situation, and he opened my eyes to all the new tax laws, investments vehicles, and strategies you can't learn in business school or with a finance degree. His dad was a multimillionaire, and all this information was common knowledge in their household. Patrick even helped me set up my first trading account, and I dipped my toe into the world of trading. Once again, I was exposed to an alternative path to wealth and success, and I started to have hope for a decent future. A *safe* future.

Eventually, I left the job as a car salesman. As usual, I wasn't focused, and I wasn't motivated to succeed in the role. It wasn't right for me. The problem was, I still needed money. The underworld was calling me back, and I felt like I had no choice but to listen. Because all my old, long-term friends, the people I grew up with, were already well and truly down that path, starting to make money and establish themselves, the call was hard to resist. The problem was, I had very few good friends in my social circle I could relate to. No one seemed interested in creating a new path, heading in a new direction. Crazy, unrealistic ideas began to manipulate my thinking. *Maybe I can make some money, invest it all, then sit back and live the good life.* At the time, it seemed like the best chance I had at creating the financial freedom I wanted. Suddenly, I was headed back down the wrong path, associating with those friends again, convinced it was all I was good for.

During this time, I was caught between two worlds. Deep down, I wanted to do what I felt was moral and ethical, but, at the same time, I lacked the self-belief I needed to commit to a better path. Importantly, I needed the easy money, so I let myself get pulled back and forth between the two worlds – the old life, old friends, and who I used to be and the new path, new possibilities, and who I *wanted* to be – not knowing where I'd eventually land.

After leaving my girlfriend from the housing commission block, along with a toxic environment and relationship, I met a new girl. She was 19 years old and someone who believed in and wanted the best for me, which, to me, was a foreign experience. She believed in me more than I believed in myself, and she couldn't have come into my life at a better time. At this point, I was starting to open my mind to new ideas, opportunities, and ventures, but I was still struggling to exercise the willpower to leave behind the people and habits of my past. They were all I knew, but suddenly I had this new light in my life, a new hope, slowly pulling me back to the right path, convincing me that I deserved better and had the potential to change. Her support was constantly at the back of my mind, influencing every decision and action. She lit a spark within me, which became a bright flame, lighting up the good in me. Later in life, that flame became a roaring fire.

During this time, I was focused on following the Rich Dad path, steering away from the underworld. I just needed that one ticket out, a clear path to a better life. I began to think like an entrepreneur, and, at age 21, I tried to start a supplement company. Unfortunately, however, I didn't have a clue what I was doing. I found a US company that sold some good fitness supplements, so I decided I'd resell their products on my website. Before I set it up, I got some legal advice, and the lawyers told me I couldn't use other people's products and relist them as mine without Australian wholesale rights to the products. That was, in fact, illegal. Apparently, they were right.

I also invested money in a hydro energy plant, but the guy running the operation turned out to be a scammer and ripped off a lot of people across the country. Another scammer, a property developer in Agnes Waters near the Great Barrier Reef, also ripped me off. I kept throwing money at investments and got burnt every time. I was young, keen, and didn't have a lot of knowledge or experience. You'd think being on the streets growing up and rubbing shoulders with some of Sydney's most known underworld figures would have made me more sceptical towards people. But I was naive, and I trusted the corporate world. I didn't believe people could get ripped off or taken advantage of – but gee was I wrong.

Even when not being scammed, doing business in the corporate world, with its complex legal system, requires a whole other skill set you may be unaware of when you start playing the game as an entrepreneur or investor. I'll discuss this more later, but I've seen people in suits who are more ruthless than street criminals. The only difference is they do it right there in the open, using legal obstacles and traps to take down the competition. Apparently, ethics aren't relevant in a legal dispute.

Between the two scam investments and all the business ideas I threw money at, I probably lost around $40K. That's a lot of money for a kid in his early 20s who, growing up, had nothing to his name. What do you think that did to my morale? It practically confirmed once again that I was right and the straight path wasn't for me. It all seemed too hard, like it was too much work, and maybe I wasn't cut out for it. Clearly, I wasn't business savvy enough to make it. I had no one to guide or mentor me and, as I didn't have my year 12 certificate, no way to get the academics I thought I needed to improve my situation. At this point in my life, success seemed further away than ever. To say I was trapped in a mental loop of negative thinking and low self-esteem would be an understatement.

At the time, I was still trying to get ahead by working a few different labour-intensive jobs, doing a lot of 12-hour days, and trying to make money the legitimate way. With all the hours I worked, I was making over $100,000 per year. It was good money, but I was paying the full $27,000 per year in tax and not smart investing. On top of that, due to trading almost all of my time to make that money, I didn't have much of a life outside of work.

I tried to be smart with any disposable income I earned but every time I chucked money at something, I got burnt. It had to be fate, right? The universe was telling me I only had one path in life and if I tried to stray from it, I'd get burnt. At that point, I didn't take much persuading. I was destined to live and die in the underworld. It was the only place that would have me, and I had to accept that fact. Everything I'd tried up to that point had failed and sent me backwards. Even though I'd been working flat out, I barely had any money in the bank and had no specific job experiences or qualifications after leaving school nearly seven years prior. Suddenly, once again, the underworld seemed like my only path to financial freedom.

Then Ricky got shot.

BIGGEST INSIGHTS FROM THE SECOND CHAPTER OF MY LIFE

Role models – It's important to consider the role models in your life, including your parents and the people you follow on social media. Who are you looking to for guidance? Pay attention to who you look up to, because they will influence your future.

Environment – I was put into Boys' Town for my benefit, to learn and grow. I was forced into that situation, but, in the real world, we need to consciously choose our environments and the people we spend time with. What environments are healthy for you and will move you towards your goals, your desired lifestyle? Those are the environments you should seek. The people and places we're exposed to can infiltrate our conscious and unconscious minds and belief systems. For the benefit of your future, it's important to safeguard your mind and only let in that which will move you closer to your goals. No one else has to walk in your shoes, so always look out for number one first.

Mentors and coaches – Beyond good role models, there's also mentors and coaches. If you can find someone with experience who can help you achieve your goals faster, it's a great investment. You could gain 10, 15, 20 years of wisdom in a much shorter timeframe, so utilise all opportunities wisely. Learning from others and avoiding their mistakes will fast-track your success.

Analyse success – The ability to analyse others' success and understand how they got there will help you find your own path forward. You'll quickly recognise that people just like you have achieved greatness through hard work, discipline, and making the right decisions. By analysing and reflecting on the success of others, you'll begin to see that a better life *is* possible, because if they can do it, you can too. It's that simple.

Build your own path to success – Once you know who you want to be and how others have achieved success, you'll need to ensure you're in the right environment and develop your own discipline, structure, and path to your goals. Yes, you should definitely learn from others, but everyone's journey is different, and you'll need to decide what yours looks like. Once you have a vision and plan, the next and most important step is to take action and follow it through.

KANE AGE 12 AT THE START OF HIGH SCHOOL

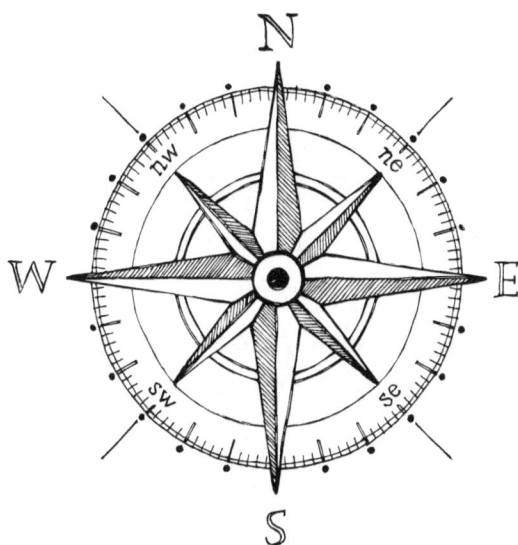

CHAPTER 3

A DRASTIC BUT NECESSARY ENVIRONMENT SHIFT

A BRUTAL ATTACK

Ricky had a pretty rough upbringing. His uncle was a bikie club member, who'd spent quite a bit of time in jail. Ricky's Dad also did a long stint in jail, so he was never around when he was growing up. A few years before I lived in the housing commission block, Ricky had lived there too. He spent the majority of his teenage years going in and out of juvenile homes, so, like me, he was on a less than ideal path through life fairly early. He was a mad bloke: jacked at 19 years old, weighing 130 kilos (most of it pure muscle), and absolutely covered in tats. Looking at him, you'd think he was born for the life he led. If anyone in that world was invincible growing up, it was Ricky. Nothing could stop the guy – or so we thought. Importantly, in my later teen years, he was one of my good mates.

Ricky and I connected at around age 16. We would train three, four, even five days a week at the PCYC. Yes, Ricky was also on the same deal with the PCYC as me and had access to the same programs. While, after meeting my new girlfriend, I started to pursue investment and entrepreneurship, looking for a way out, Ricky was always committed to the street life. He never flinched from it, and I don't think he ever had a legitimate job.

Even when I tried to distance myself from that path, Ricky and others were always on the outskirts of my life, ready for a catch up or to help with any situation. Was it a healthy friendship circle? Not at all, especially if I wanted to change for the better or live on the straight and narrow, but they were still my friends. I frequently tried to close myself off from that world and those relationships, but I always found myself back in contact, usually ending up out at the pub or clubs. Deep down, I knew that life wasn't for me – it didn't feel right – but, time and time again, disconnecting from my past proved difficult.

Inevitably, shit went sideways, as it always does when you're living that life. It's never a matter of if but *when*. We all thought Ricky was unstoppable, and so did he, which led to him getting in over his head. That's when I got the phone call. Ricky had been stabbed multiple times, and, for good measure, they shot him two times, one in the head, another in the neck. I get it – a big boy like that, you want to make sure he's not getting back up. It was a brutal attack.

The thing is, he did get back up. Adrenaline kicked in, and he managed to run away, bleeding from multiple stab wounds, a bullet lodged in his head. He fled his attackers and made it 15 minutes down the road to the highway, where he finally collapsed in front of a moving car. Thankfully, the car didn't hit him, and the driver stopped and called an ambulance.

When Ricky arrived at hospital, they rushed him to emergency, where he died on the operating table – for about 40 seconds. Miraculously, they managed to resuscitate him and keep him alive. The doctors said it was likely all of the steroids and growth hormones that had saved him. Like I said, we all thought Ricky was unstoppable, and he'd just gone and proven us right.

Once he was awake, he called me, laughing. I distinctly recall the conversation. In a deep voice, he announced, "I'm the white 50 Cent!" Although he was laughing about the incident, I later learnt he was actually quite traumatised. Who wouldn't be? But he tried to brush it off and act as if almost dying like that wasn't a big deal. To Ricky, growing up the way he did, that life and everything that came with it were the norm. If you're being realistic, you expect to get shot or stabbed at some point. Like I said, it's only a matter of when. If it could happen to Ricky, it could – and likely *would* – happen to me. Wrong place, wrong time – that's all it would take for my time to come.

Was that the life I wanted? Was that who I wanted to be? Did I want to spend the rest of my life looking over my shoulder, wondering if today was the day? With the money and excitement came the risk, the risk to not only my life but to the lives of my family as well. It wasn't what I signed up for. I was a young man, 22 years old, and I still had a lot to learn and experience. There had to be more to life. Others had found better paths, so why couldn't I?

It was time for me to make a drastic but necessary change in my life.

DANNY AND BEAU

After Ricky's near-death experience, I knew I had to get out. That wasn't what I signed up for. I didn't know how, and I didn't know what I'd do, but I knew I couldn't keep living like that, with one foot in the ordinary world and the other in the under-world. Over the course of the next few months, I tried to figure out what I'd do. I tried to find a way out. *How can I create a better life for myself?* Finally, I found the answer.

Two of my good mates, Danny and Beau – who I'd known from around age 13 but had become a lot closer with from age 19 – had left town to work in the mines. They were my two normal friends, who did normal things. They weren't associated with that other world. They were just a couple of good guys, who generally did the right thing. Yes, they still went out, partied, and had fun, but, on Monday mornings, they showed up to work and worked hard to earn an honest living. They had goals and worked to achieve them. Importantly, they weren't the sorts of people I usually associated with, which was something that drew me to them. They inspired me to set goals and work hard, and hanging out with them felt safe and right.

Danny and Beau were people I could trust. They were genuine mates, who I could have fun with but also be real with. Unlike many of the other people in my life, they cared about me and the decisions I made. They wanted what was best for me, and vice versa. Danny and Beau were some of the only people in my life who seemed to be heading in the right direction. I knew I could never truly trust the people in my other life. They could never be a core group of real friends. I wouldn't trust most of them to look after my dog, let alone want my kids growing up around them. It may sound harsh, but it's true. It was the reality of the situation.

I'm not saying Danny and Beau never had it rough. They both grew up in lower-income families, were raised by single mums, and were in or associated with the housing commission system. However, they chose to work hard, and they avoided getting caught up in any of the sketchy business I was around.

Danny bought his first unit when he was 21. Coming from a poor background, that's a big accomplishment. How did he do it? One, he worked hard. Two, he was an absolute tight-arse. If we ever went out to dinner, he'd always eat a big bowl of rice and corned beef beforehand and not order any food while out. Then he'd finish everyone else's leftovers. He never spent money if he didn't have to, and, by the age of 21, he had a good 100 grand in the bank. When Danny bought his unit, Beau moved in with him and paid rent.

They were great guys, great friends. I felt a real sense of camaraderie with them, and they never judged me for who I was. They never spoke of my other life because they didn't care. They liked me for who I was outside of that life; they liked me for me, which was a breath of fresh air. I could be myself, the real Kane. I didn't have to put on and maintain a tough-guy front. It had been a long time since I could be vulnerable around other people.

With all the compounding bullshit in my life – Ricky getting shot, no genuine career or direction, being broke and in debt, surrounded by idiots – I had to find a way out through any means necessary, even if it meant making a drastic change and taking a wild leap. I had a great girlfriend, who cared about me, and I needed to start making good, sensible decisions, for me and for her. I had to decide who I wanted to surround myself with and what I wanted my future to look like.

When Danny and Beau left for the mines, I asked them, "Can you get me in too?" I didn't say why I wanted to leave, but they knew I was desperate. With them gone, I'd have no sensible mates around me, no good influences, and I foresaw what that would lead to. So, I didn't directly state my reasons for wanting to leave, and they never directly asked. They knew I needed to get away, and, as good mates do, they agreed to help.

WHY ME? WHY YOU? WHY ANYONE?

Even though Danny, Beau, and I had similarly rough upbringings, we went down different paths. They worked to get ahead, whereas I struggled to hold a job or find any direction in life. They lived relatively normal lives, whereas I was turning to a life of crime. So, what was so different between me and them? What made me wander down the dark path, while they trekked towards a brighter future? What dictates the direction anyone takes in life?

I honestly think my environment and the people I hung around with were a big influence. Danny and Beau met each other fairly young and became good mates. Early on, they supported each other, and they didn't end up having the trouble at school I had. As we know, whenever I was suspended, I'd hang out in the streets with other juvenile delinquents. *They* were my friends. *They* were my influences. *They* were my social support. It's a bit of a farce, isn't it? We force the naughty kids together, separating them from the good kids, and they end up learning each other's bad habits. Where's the logic in that?

And we *are* creatures of habit. The thing is, most habits form unconsciously. Environment, people, and life events all work to impact our behaviours in the short and long term and if we're not paying attention to how these elements affect us, resisting their influence is difficult.

THAT'S A FACT

Research shows that developing a new habit or routines takes 66 days on average. For some people, habits develop much sooner; for others, a behaviour can take over 200 days to become habitual.[9] The timeframe depends on the individual and the practiced behaviour or task.

For an action to become habitual, you must perform it regularly and consistently over time. Eventually, the habit will embed itself in your subconscious and become automatic.

So, don't think you can change your automatic behaviour overnight. In most cases, you're in for at least a few good weeks of dedication and persistence before you start noticing results – so keep at it. It *will* get easier, and the effort will be well worth the reward.

Look at your closest five friends – they're likely having the biggest influence on your life right now. In fact, whatever path they're going down is probably where you're headed too, for better or worse. The people who you surround yourself with rub off on you. If you're aware of this, you can better control *how much* they influence your decisions and behaviours, but good luck avoiding their influence altogether. That's why it's important to surround yourself with the *right* people in the right environment. I'm not just talking about your physical environment, either.

More and more, we're living our lives online, and the things we read on social media and elsewhere absolutely impact the way we think, feel, and behave. We can't choose the family or circumstances we're born into, but we *can* decide who we hang out with outside of work and school. We *can* choose the content we consume, whether online, in books, or elsewhere. While we rarely have complete control over our environments or the people we associate with, we *can* control a lot of what we expose ourselves too, but we have to be aware and willing to put in the effort.

Most big achievements don't happen by chance. If you want to walk the road to success, you have to put yourself on it. Don't wait for fate or others to steer you in the right direction – because you'll die waiting. Instead, start taking the steps necessary to get to where you want to go. Mostly, the journey involves a series of small steps, but sometimes you'll need to take a giant leap.

One of the keys to reaching your goals is surrounding yourself with like-minded people who want to achieve the same things. It's a big part of why I built the True North Academy. Not only are our members learning how to develop goals, improve their finances, and create better lifestyles, but they also get exposed to others who are on the same path – or want to get on it. Whether they're ready to take the next step or the first step of their journeys, I help them identify the *right* step to take. If I'd had a solid community around me when I was trying to figure it all out, without a doubt, I would've had a much smoother ride to success. Unfortunately, as you'll soon learn, I had to do it the hard way.

NEW ENVIRONMENT, NEW STRUGGLES

I knew a job in the mines was my ticket out of the life I was living, but the problem was, I didn't know anything about mining. I didn't have any experience, and I didn't have the tickets needed to work in a mine. So, what was the solution? Danny and Beau found a job for me as a yardie, working for a scaffolding company at an open-cut mine in the Northern Territory. The gig required very little experience and few qualifications, just a forklift license, which I had. Normally, they hired locally for the job; they didn't fly people in for it, but they were having trouble finding local talent for a job that didn't exactly require a lot of talent, so they took me on with a fly-in fly-out arrangement.

If you've worked in the mines or know someone who has, you probably know that the money can be quite good. For me, however, that wasn't the case. Considering the long hours and labour-intensive work, the money wasn't great. On top of that, I was a lowly yardie, so the scaffolders would hang shit on me all day long, which was a little tough to deal with, but I sucked it up and got on with the job. Here I was, working 12-hour days in the scorching heat for average pay – I could've easily made the same money labouring back in Sydney, with the luxury of going home and actually having something to do on weekends besides looking at red dirt. Luckily, because I spent so much time at work and lived onsite, my expenses were low, and I managed to save a lot of what I earned. Importantly, I'd achieved the drastic environment shift I needed.

During this time, I really started to practise the art of discipline, and I was actively setting and working towards goals to create a better future. Because my expenses were low, my bank balance grew, and I had to decide how to capitalise on the situation *without* being burnt by another scam artist. The bus ride from my accommodation to the mine was about 30 minutes each way. Combine that with two 45-minute smoko breaks each day due to the long shifts, free time in the evenings, and getting every second Sunday off due to exhaustion and safety risks, and I had plenty of time to think, read, and plan for the future. I focused on who I wanted to be, where I wanted to be, and how I was going to get there. Over time, I recreated myself, reprogramming my brain and adjusting my thoughts and behaviours to match the lifestyle I wanted to achieve. Essentially, I was starting from the bottom, and I knew I had a long way to go, but I'd already taken the first step to a better life.

Of course, there were people from that other world who weren't supportive of my decision. But whenever I was back in Sydney, I just kept my head down and went about my life. I didn't associate with those people anymore, and I didn't let myself get pulled back into that world. Sure, I was kicking shit and doing hard, menial labour in the desert, but I was relatively safe, and now I had a clear head and the ability to think and plan. The job sucked, but it was a way out, a stepping stone to something bigger and better – or so I hoped.

THAT'S A FACT

Your inner circle matters. Friends, family, classmates, colleagues – whoever you associate with the most will influence your thoughts, beliefs, values, and actions. The people closest to you have the potential to either steer you towards success or away from it, affecting your happiness, quality of life, and relationships.[10]

For me, Danny and Beau were the positive people I needed in my circle. We became the best of friends and naturally influenced one another to grow together and chase our dreams. Taking the journey with great, like-minded people, who will prop you up rather than bring you down, makes it so much more fulfilling. I'll say it again – *your inner circle matters*.

QUESTION EVERYTHING (EVEN THIS STATEMENT)

Have you heard about the experiment with the monkeys and the ladder? Humour me. I swear it relates to what we've been talking about: habits, learnt behaviour, and nonsensical systems and rules.

In the experiment, researchers place five monkeys in a cage, with a ladder in the middle that leads to a bunch of bananas. Whenever a monkey tries to climb the ladder, the researchers spray them all with cold water, which they're not really into. Eventually, some of the monkeys get fed up with the constant soaking, so they stop going for the bananas at the top of the ladder or stop going near the ladder at all. If any other monkey attempts to climb the ladder, the others respond and try to stop him. Soon, no one even goes for the bananas anymore. It's not worth the struggle.

THAT'S A FACT

Did you know that monkeys don't actually eat bananas in the wild? That's right – we've been fed a lie! That's not to say monkeys don't enjoy a banana or two when they can get their hands on them, but it's not a food they typically encounter in the wild.[11] Although most of us don't give a shit about the diet of a monkey, it's a good lesson in questioning everything you've ever been taught. Sometimes, we're walking around believing a lie.

Next, the researchers remove one monkey and replace it with a fresh one. Naturally, the newbie tries to climb the ladder, but the others quickly stop him, throwing him to the ground and attacking him out of fear, a fear that only the original monkeys understand. The newbie now knows the ladder is off limits, but he doesn't know why. Researchers repeat the process of replacing the original monkeys with others, each newbie quickly learning not to mess with the ladder.

Eventually, none of the original monkeys remain, yet no one dares go for the bananas. They don't understand why none of them will even attempt to climb the ladder anymore but they know that if they go near it, they're in for a beating. That's the way it has been from the beginning, since they joined the group. Everyone knows the ladder is forbidden. But *why* is it forbidden? The problem is, the monkeys don't challenge the status quo, and many humans fall into the same trap. None of the monkeys have even experienced being sprayed with the water, but they've fallen in line with the culture within the cage. They're accepted that the rules are the rules, even if they don't know why they exist, even if they don't make sense.

To an extent, we're all monkeys in a cage. There are so many rules and systems in place that don't make a lot of sense when you really start to analyse them, but we've been conditioned to accept them. Do the eggs at home go in the cupboard or the fridge? Some people say cupboard; others say fridge. Why? Because they're likely doing whatever their parents did, which is an unconscious behaviour that came from *their* parents, and so on.

Our closest circle of people (or monkeys) can have a massive influence on our behaviours, which is why surrounding ourselves with the *right* people is important. The behaviours we unconsciously adopt can be the most dangerous, as they quietly enter our lives and can shift our thinking without us realising. How often do we stop and ask, "Is this right?" You notice these little learnt behaviours more when you move in with a partner. Likely, you both have different ways of doing things based on what your household did growing up. There's nothing wrong with that, but it's important to recognise that some of our behaviours aren't logical. Some of society's rules aren't logical. Some of the systems we live our lives by don't make sense.

The education system, the financial system, our system of government – do *they* make sense? Is this the best we can do? Or are we simply carrying on a tradition? Are we merely slaves to the culture we were born into? I'm not saying every rule or system is bullshit, but I *am* saying we should be questioning everything and forming our own conclusions.

The first step to breaking a bad habit is recognising that it exists. The next step is to decondition yourself and replace that bad habit with better ones.

WHO DO YOU NEED TO BECOME?

At the end of the day, humans are pack animals. We need to be in a community; we need to have a social group, and we need to feel accepted. It's hardwired into us. We need to be part of a tribe. In the tribal days, we all lived in small groups. If you were outcast from the tribe, it practically meant death, which is why we're so anxious to fit in and feel accepted by the people around us.

That's what I found in the underworld: acceptance. It didn't matter that I hadn't finished high school, didn't have a great job, and had spent most of my teenage years fucking up. In that world, I felt accepted. I felt understood. I felt like I fit in. I was a part of the tribe. Because my sense of self-worth had eroded over time, naturally, I never considered doing anything great with my life. I always had a low standard for myself. It was an unconscious belief created by the series of unfortunate events and poor decisions from my youth, later fuelled by having the wrong circle of people around me. Thankfully, I caught it before

I went too far down the wrong path and there was no turning back.

For me to do that drastic environment shift, I had to cast myself out of the tribe. I had to separate myself from the only group I felt like I'd ever belonged to. That shit isn't easy. But I knew, if I wanted a better life, I didn't have a choice. Trust me, disengaging from negative people, environments, and situations is something you need to be able to handle if you want to be successful. On my own path to success, I've had to level up and become a better version of myself several times now. In the process, I've had to cut people out of my life who've projected their negativity and insecurities onto me. It's never easy to cut people from your circle – at least, it hasn't been for me – but, at times, it's absolutely necessary. I can't stress this enough.

When you do a big environment shift, you leave a lot behind. You leave behind all the people who inadvertently pushed you in that new direction. When this happens, you also need people pulling you forward. For me, those people were Danny and Beau. They pulled me towards a new environment, new opportunities, a new community, a new tribe. Before you start cutting off friends, you need to have support in place. You need to have a new tribe that's ready and willing to take you in. Otherwise, you're in for a sad and lonely time. Likely, you'll be tempted to return to your old tribe because that's where the comfort and support is. Your old life will keep calling you back.

The key is to find new friends who are more aligned with your interests and the direction you want to go. While I made a pretty abrupt decision to leave for the mines, I had good support in Danny and Beau. Without them, I don't know where I would've ended up. It's important to remember that your friends don't have to live *your* life. You do. If someone isn't pushing you closer to your goals and the person you want to be, you may need to cut them off. Yes, I felt bad about cutting off people I'd known my whole life, or for many years, but, at the end of the day, they didn't have to walk in my shoes and deal with the consequences of my actions. You have to make decisions that benefit *you*. When you lie down at night, you're the one who has to deal with your thoughts and your conscience around the decisions you've made. There's no one else, no one to blame; it's just you. No one else can carry that burden. If changing your circle or environment is the right decision for you, then that's what you need to do. It's what I had to do.

Some people, no matter how long you've known them, may no longer be aligned with you and where you want to go in life. As we grow up and mature, many of us get long-term partners and start families. If we've got single friends who are still out partying every weekend, finding common ground is difficult, and we often drift apart. Look, there's nothing wrong with either lifestyle if that's what you want to do, but it doesn't matter if you've known someone since high school or even earlier. There's no point holding on to the past if it's going to fuck up your future. It's that simple.

When we start moving towards success, it's often not just our circles and environments that need to change. *We* need to change too. We have to become different people. I'm not who I was 10 years ago, let alone who I was 15 or 20 years ago, by a long shot. My attitude, my behaviour, my mindset, my way of thinking have all changed. I've made sacrifices, and I've taken on big responsibilities. If I were still out partying every night, I wouldn't have been able to hack the difficult path I eventually chose and built.

If the person you are now isn't capable of success, then that person needs to change. I'm not saying you need to change who you are deep down, but you can adjust your attitude, your behaviour, and the way you operate to have the best chance of reaching your goals. What are you trying to achieve? What sort of person do you need to be to achieve it? That's who you must become.

As mentioned in chapter one, in my Financial Foundations course, the first step to achieving your financial goals is to develop your vision. What's the life you want to create? It's hard to get to your destination if you don't know where you're trying to go, right? Once you're clear on the four pillars of your overall vision – personal life, business or career, relationships, health – we then identify your values and beliefs. These are important! They'll be your compass for your entire journey, ensuring you stay true to who you are (or who you want to become). As we know, money can change people, often not for the better. Finally, we break down each vision into goals and identify the steps required to reach them. Simple, right? It's both holistic *and* logical. Once you're clear on your vision, values and beliefs, goals, and the necessary steps, you can dive into learning the practical finance skills you'll use to make it all happen.

The main point I want to make is, gaining clarity around your vision is one of the most important steps to success. However, if you want to change yourself, your situation, and the world around you, you must be 100 percent clear on your values and your beliefs. They will be your North Star.

YOU'RE NOT STUCK

Guess what? You're not stuck. You're not stuck in your environment, in your circle, in your job, in your mindset. Whatever's holding you back – *you're not stuck*. It may *feel* like you're stuck, but you're not.

In my mind, I was stuck for so long: stuck in the environment I'd grown up in, stuck with the crew I was hanging out with, stuck with the fate I thought I deserved. It wasn't until I took that massive step to unstick myself, leaving for the mines, that I realised I wasn't as stuck as I thought I was. In fact, I had all the freedom in the world. Sure, I was broke, in debt, and had no notable qualifications, but I was still free to try to better my situation.

When we're babies, we don't have a lot of freedom. If our home situation sucks, we can't just get up and walk away. We can't really change anything. We can't look at our parents and say, "The way you're letting me cry myself to sleep every night, that's bullshit, and you know it. If something doesn't change, I'm out of here." As babies, or even young children, we don't have that sort of freedom. We can't control what happens to us when we're kids. It's a hard fact of life.

I talk to kids all the time who've come from broken families and faced serious adversity. Their environments and upbringings shaped a lot of their behaviours, but they didn't choose to start life this way. They just had to accept the cards they were dealt. Is it fair? Hell no. Is it the end of the world? Absolutely not. As you mature, you become more capable of conscious change. At a certain point, you can no longer blame the system, your parents, or anybody else but yourself. It's a tough reality to accept, but it's the hard truth.

You can't change the past, but, once you become aware of the negative influences in your life, you can take ownership of the future. You can take responsibility for what you do and where you go next. Your past and your past conditioning don't have to rule you for the rest of your life. You can decide, right now, to say, "I choose to not live a life of suffering anymore." The suffering doesn't need to continue, but you must decide you're going to change and then take action to make that change.

I once did a big presentation at the police academy in Goulburn, New South Wales, explaining why some of us, as youths, act out and seem angry and violent. Using the analogy of an abused dog, I helped the youth officers understand what the kids they're dealing with are going through.

Whatever you expose a dog to determines its temperament and behaviour. For instance, imagine that you go to the pound and find a little fox terrier, anxious and shaking in the corner of its cage. You can tell just by looking at it that it's disturbed. When you go to pat the dog, it tries to bite you out of fear. Was it born scared? Of course not. Something must have happened in its past to make it react that way. The environment in which it grew up traumatised it in some way, causing it to become more aggressive. It has been living in fear for so long that it has turned vicious. Is it the dog's fault? No way. It couldn't control who owned it. Even so, it's stuck with the conditioning created by its previous environment.

Luckily, it's not a big dog, so it's not going to cause too much damage when it lashes out. You can work with a dog like that, slowly getting it to trust you so you can undo its conditioning. If it's a big dog, well, you're in for even more of a challenge. Either way, the process isn't easy; it takes a lot of work from both parties, but it can be done. In fact, it *should* be done. That's what I wanted those youth officers to understand.

Someone might be a violent person, a drug addict, a criminal – but why? Wouldn't any one of us go down the same path if we grew up under the exact same conditions as that person? We can argue nature versus nurture all day long, but there's no denying that our environments and early conditioning play a massive role in who we become and how we interact with the world. It's easy to blame people for who and where they are in life without understanding where they've come from. It's a big factor we can't overlook.

Yes, at a certain point, we need to take responsibility for our own lives and make positive changes. But sometimes there's a lot of damage to undo, and some of us are so entrenched in our current behaviours that we can't see a way forward. Some of us don't have the knowledge and understanding required to find a better path, and we need a little – or, let's be honest, a *lot* of – help to start making positive changes.

When I was living in housing commission, I saw kids exposed to horrific things, really messed up stuff that no one, let alone a child, should have to experience. We're all going to experience bad shit in our lives, some of us worse than others, but we can't spend our lives making excuses. We're not stuck in the past. Or at least, we don't have to be. We all have the power to take control of our lives. Don't let the trauma and adversity you've faced hold you down. When you believe you're permanently stuck in a situation, taking action to move forward is difficult. Why bother if it won't lead anywhere?

I've seen this same mindset in action when people get into serious debt. They feel so overwhelmed, overloaded, and hopeless that they can't imagine a way out, so they don't even try to take the steps to put themselves in a better financial position. They just keep spending. Why budget and put money aside if you're never going to clear that debt? You might as well make yourself feel good with a new pair of shoes or the latest gaming console or an expensive meal, right? They seek short-term gratification because they feel stuck in the long-term, but it's this mindset, this self-fulfilling prophecy that causes them to remain in their current, shitty situations.

To start making positive changes, you have to believe you can escape your current circumstances. It's why I wanted to share my story – to show you that it *is* possible. If I can do it and others can too, why not you? Why not anyone who's out there struggling and feeling stuck? Honestly, a lack of belief is one of the biggest barriers to a better life. Of course, it's not the only barrier, but it's undeniably massive for a lot of people, myself included.

When I left for the mines, I effectively unstuck myself, but that didn't mean I couldn't get pulled back into the same old way of operating. Changing my environment was the first step. Next, I had to figure out where to go from there. At the time, I never would've guessed that I'd end up where I did. The thing is, moving to the mines and proving that I could actually achieve something boosted my self-belief. *Okay, I did this. What else can I do?* Even small wins create momentum, and once you start to gain traction, moving forward gets a lot easier. Whatever you need to do to stoke your self-belief – do it. You just need someone to believe in you, give you hope, tell you it's okay, and say you are worthy and can become more than you are today.

To you and everyone else reading this book – you can do more. You're more than capable of achieving great things. You just need to get clear on what those things are and take action. Every great journey starts with one step forward.

"A boy comes to me with a spark of interest. I feed the spark and it becomes a flame. I feed the flame and it becomes a fire. I feed the fire and it becomes a roaring blaze."
– CUS D'AMATO, MIKE TYSON'S COACH, GUARDIAN, AND FATHER FIGURE

Looking back, both the teenage and 20-something-year-old me let the world limit their beliefs so much. Yes, you've got to be realistic with your goals; otherwise, you're setting yourself up for failure and disappointment, but you've also got to have a healthy level of self-belief. While self-belief *is* important, it will only get you so far. You also need to have a clear vision, a plan, and be prepared to do the work. However, without self-belief and self-worth, you'll struggle to imagine a brighter future – it won't seem possible – and you'll be unlikely to get there. If you don't think a better life is possible, I'm here to tell you you're wrong. I can talk the talk because I've walked the walk.

When I made the tough decision to abandon my old life, I took a big step in the right direction. However, I still had a lot of work ahead of me if I truly wanted to break free from my past.

For me, the struggle was far from over.

BIGGEST INSIGHTS FROM THE THIRD CHAPTER OF MY LIFE

Write your own life story – Life isn't about what happens to you, as my story shows. For so many years, I played the victim – the school was against me; Dad wasn't around, and I was from a lower-class family. But then I saw Danny and Beau, who were both from similar households, and my perceptions began to change. They could've ended up worse off than me, but they didn't accept their positions in life. They weren't looking for excuses or shortcuts. They didn't subscribe to the victim mentality. From them, I learnt that what happens to us doesn't decide our future. It only makes up our past. You get to decide the story you want to live. Do you want to be the victim? Or do you want to be the hero? Do you want to be the one who breaks free and says, "Fuck it! I'm not settling for my current life story. I want more, and I deserve more"? The choice is yours.

Change requires sacrifice – The new path you choose to walk may not be easy. For me, it required leaving my hometown in Sydney, isolating myself in a mining camp in the desert, and creating new habits, routines, and rituals. I had to leave behind the person I was and create a new version of myself. My new environment helped me build positive habits around healthy eating, exercise, and continuous self-improvement. With a healthy body, I had a clear mind and could stay focused on my goals. Because my expenses were low, I was able to save money. Because I had so much free time, I was able to read, study, and learn new skills, which turned out to be an important, initial step in a much larger journey. Sometimes those first steps aren't the most exciting, but they're a start, and they're necessary. Don't let your ego tell you otherwise. Creating change requires sacrifice, but, in the end, the reward is well worth it.

Don't be afraid to cut people loose – Letting go of friends, and sometimes family, is a difficult but often necessary part of changing your lifestyle. On my journey, I left many lifelong friends behind. We had history, great memories, and we were in the trenches together, but, at a certain point, I decided my future was more important than old friendships. Those friends I left behind weren't going to pay my rent or mortgage, put food on my table, or build a better future for my kids. Don't get me wrong – I didn't cut all my lifelong mates loose. There are a few who came from the same places as me and are still in my life today, and we're extremely close. They also changed along the way, and our values and lives aligned. The key is to pick the right people to take the journey with, those who want the best for you, just as you'd want the best for them.

Do what's right for you – Just because a friend made money through cryptocurrency or a dropshipping business, it doesn't mean those ventures are right for you. Be wary of what people are trying to sell you. The sharks are out there, and I've been bitten several times over, learning the hard way not to believe everything I hear. In the world of social media, you'll see promises that are absolute bullshit and not worth the time it takes to read them. That doesn't mean you should ignore good opportunities, but you must be ready to ask questions, challenge any claims, and adequately assess the situation. Don't be too gullible. Don't fall for a slick sales pitch. Don't do anything that doesn't align with your vision, values, and goals.

Do it for future you – Break free from your current mindset and focus on the future you – at age 40, 50, or retired at 65. If you can't do it for yourself, do it for your kids, if that's what you see in your future. Leverage your vision of the future to pull yourself out of where you are today towards your future self. When making any change, big or small, focus on the first steps first. Makes sense, right? Yes, you may have a lofty goal or dream for your life, but you'll struggle to get there if you aren't focused on the next step. The others will come eventually.

Be flexible – To get to where you want to go, you must be able to adapt. If you map out 50 steps over ten years to achieve your dream lifestyle, your situation could change within the first three steps. Then where does that leave you? With a map that's no longer relevant. Your overall vision may not change, but the steps you take to achieve it likely will. Flexibility and adaptability are important.

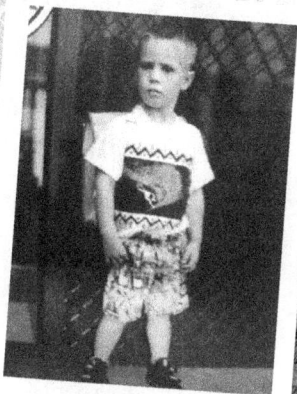

KANE FIRST DAY
PRESCHOOL

KANE AFTER BREAKING DISTRICT 100M
SPRINT RECORD BY 1.5 SECONDS

KANE AFTER COMING SECOND IN
NIPPERS STATE BEACH SPRINT

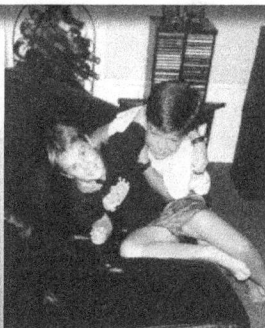

KANE AND JON THE
GREEK BOTH AGE 6

KANE AGE 12 LIVING WITH MUM IN
UNCLE'S GRANNY FLAT WHILE MUM
UNDERGOES CHEMO

KANE 18 YEARS OLD LIVING IN BACK ROOM
WITH A BED SHEET HUNG FOR PRIVACY

KANE AGE 21 BEFORE DECIDING
TO GO TO THE MINES

KANE'S FIRST YEAR AWAY
SCAFFOLDING IN MINES

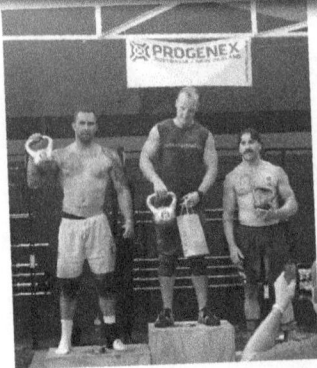
KANE MINING IN ORANGE NSW

KANE AFTER PLACING SECOND
AT CROSSFIT COMP IN SYDNEY

KANE AFTER BECOMING
A PARTNER

KANE'S OFFICE WHILE
PARTNERING WITH RUSSELL

KANE, BEAU, DANNY, AND KRIS –
CLOSEST FRIENDS GROWING UP

FIRST INVESTMENT PROPERTY
RENOVATION IN ORANGE – BEFORE

FIRST INVESTMENT PROPERTY
RENOVATION IN ORANGE – AFTER

BALI DURING
SPIRITUAL JOURNEY

KANE AT THE GREAT
WALL OF CHINA

KANE (A CHANGED
MAN) AND MUM

TRAVELLING THROUGH BALI BEFORE
STARTING TRUE NORTH

OZTAG GRAND FINAL WIN

KANE WITH FOSTER KID DYLAN
AGE 18 AND HIS COUSIN CHRIS

YOUTH TALK TO YOUNG GIRLS AT PCYC

TOUGH MUDDER WITH PCYC
PROGRAM KIDS

TALK AT BOYS' TOWN

TALKING AT BOYS' TOWN

SCHOOL TALK

KANE AFTER BUYING A HOMELESS
MAN NEW SHOES AND A WARM MEAL

FAMILY PHOTO

SUTHERLAND TO SHIRE EVENT
FOR THE BUSINESS

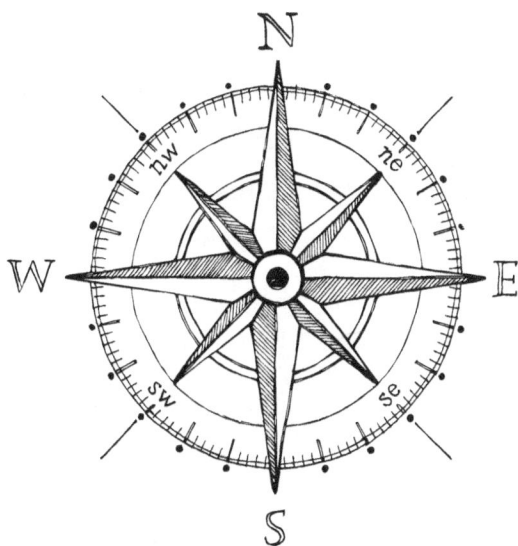

CHAPTER 4

MINER BY DAY, TRADER BY NIGHT

WE ALL HAVE ROLES TO PLAY

When you need to make a drastic, life-changing decision, it helps when you feel like you have no other options. That's how I felt when I went to the mines. Either I left Sydney, or I'd eventually end up in jail or die in the streets, like so many had before me. The thing is, I didn't know what I'd do once I got to the mines. Yes, I'd work hard and, for the first time in my life, try not to complain too much, but I didn't want to grow old in the desert, working in a mine until I retired. That's not a dig at miners, retired or otherwise. Many of them work hard and live fulfilling lives. However, for many who'd been at it long-term, there were too many divorces, too much time spent away from their kids, too much drinking, smoking, and gambling. Basically, all the money they made went out the door as quickly as it came in, leaving them in a constant cycle of needing to earn more to support their expensive lifestyles.

We all have our roles to play in this life, and I knew I wasn't meant to be a miner long-term. The job was a stepping stone to being an entrepreneur, an investor, or a business guy, just like in *Rich Dad Poor Dad*, where the father figure with no education learnt how money worked and made a good living through applied knowledge.

While I knew I had a bigger role to play, at the time, I didn't know exactly what it would be.

SUCCESS REQUIRES SACRIFICE

When I left Sydney, I wasn't just abandoning my old life, my underworld friends, and my family; I was also leaving a girlfriend behind.

Dana was different from those I'd dated in the past. What do I mean? She came from a good family, had a good upbringing, and mostly had her head screwed on right. She taught me a lot of normal social behaviours and, through her mum's and stepdad's relationship, showed me what a healthy household looked like. They were a caring, loving family. And here I was – the shitbag kid.

Leaving Dana behind was the most difficult part of the move, but, as we know, I'd reached a pivotal moment in my life, and staying wasn't an option. So, I left her for weeks at a time, returning during my off week, but long-distance relationships are always hard, and it was never going to work. We were together for around eight years before we finally split up.

Even though our relationship didn't survive the mines, Dana played an important part in my life and my decision to leave to create a better future. She was a really caring person, and she helped me develop self-belief and entertain the possibility of becoming something better than what I was when we first met. She saw beyond the version of me that was getting into trouble, walking down a dark path, and she convinced me of my worth. She did this indirectly, mind you. It wasn't like she sat me down and told me I was good; she just made me feel like I was good enough. Dana saw a better person in me. She saw that I had a good heart and a good head on my shoulders, and these beliefs reflected back at me, helping me see them for myself. She knew I didn't belong with the people I was associating with at the time. Although she was always respectful to those friends, I know she didn't like me being around them.

Essentially, Dana saw my potential and helped me see it too.

Having people like that in our lives is so important. They can change the way we think, the way we feel, and the overall direction we're headed in life.

THE LIFE OF A MINER IS ROUGH

Away from the noise of Sydney, I could think clearly. Being in the middle of the desert, no one from my old life could just drop around and pull me back onto the bad path. Finally, I could figure out what the best version of me looked like and what I needed to do to become that person.

By day, I was too busy to get into trouble. At the mine where I worked, we refined bauxite into alumina, which would become aluminium. The refining process involved massive tanks, caustic soda, and insane temperatures, over 200°C – as if it wasn't already hot enough in the desert.

We carried caustic emergency packs with us at all times because if a drop of the chemical got on our skin, it would burn through the flesh before we'd even felt it. Sometimes, pipes would leak or burst, or valves would fail, so we all had to be on high alert. It was a brutal job. Combine the constant hazards with the harsh desert sun, and we were basically living in hell. But it was still better than the alternative: living and eventually dying in the underworld. In that old life, I was destined for destruction. Now, at least I had a chance.

For the most part, I just put my head down, got the work done, and hit the gym in my downtime. Once again, I had routine and structure, similar to what I experienced at Boys' Town. Although we worked brutally long days, I still had plenty of free time in the evenings and while travelling to and from the mine site each day. As mentioned, I also had the odd Sunday off for safety reasons. With so much time to kill, I soon discovered the power of self-education, which I charged into like a bull.

SELF-EDUCATE YOUR WAY TO SUCCESS

When you're stuck in the desert for weeks at a time, you miss a lot: birthdays, parties, weddings, births, and the fun things some young ones live for, like festivals – all the big events, right? By day, you're out there in long overalls, 40-degree heat, high humidity, just sweating your arsehole out. In a 12-hour shift, we'd need to replace our overalls twice, during each of our two breaks, due to the amount of sweat. By the time we changed them, they'd be completely wet, which could cause a mean heat rash. So, twice per shift, we swapped into fresh overalls and tossed the old, sweaty ones into the onsite washing machine. Yep, it's a tough life.

To stay sane in that environment, I needed to do more than just work and workout. I had to find a way to keep moving myself forward, a new way of thinking. I had to reprogram myself, my mind, my thoughts, and create new behaviours and habits. I still had a lot of bad habits to break and new ones to create. While I could – and did – move up the ranks in the mine and earn a decent wage, I didn't want to be stuck there for the rest of my life. Like I said, it wasn't the role I felt I was meant to play in the long term, especially if I wanted a life where I could be home with my friends, girlfriend, and family.

How could I continue to improve the quality of my life? What did I need to learn? *How* could I learn it? The education system had failed me, as it does so many. *Rich Dad Poor Dad* was constantly at the forefront of my mind. I'd come to the crossroad, and I'd chosen the path to a good life. But what did that path mean now that I was on it? What would I need to do to keep moving forward?

Thinking about *Rich Dad Poor Dad*, I realised that books could be both cheap and educational, and, even though I hated school, I didn't mind reading. The right books wouldn't just give me the knowledge I needed to better my situation, but they'd give me important insights too. Everyone we meet has something to teach us – for real. I truly believe that. Even children have something to teach us. People like Richard Branson were really big on talking to kids because they're generally more creative than adults. Why? Because they don't see the limitations we're conditioned to accept as adults. They have unbound creativity, and they see things we can't. Everyone has a unique understanding of the world, and, in a way, the authors of the books I read became my mentors. As I said, there weren't many good people in my life who were on the same path as me and could help guide me to where I wanted to go, so books became my teachers. When I read, I felt like the authors were talking directly to me, teaching me, sharing their life's insights and sometimes their greatest work, and I'd take it all on board. I'd absorb everything and then write it down on paper. Journalling became a way of debating, reciting, or memorising the information I consumed day to day.

"My attitude has always been, if you fall flat on your face, at least you're moving forward. All you have to do is get back up and try again."
– RICHARD BRANSON

I took every opportunity to read and learn as much as I could. I read on the bus to work, on my lunch breaks, in my room at night, on the plane trips to Sydney and back, immersing myself in other people's knowledge and experiences. The books I read weren't like textbooks, nothing that dense. They were more like biographies, people's lived experiences intertwined with wisdom and practical advice, much like this book. The best authors don't just explain what they did (what to do) to achieve success; they also discuss the times when they fucked up (what not to do) so we don't have to make the same mistakes. They share their successes and the journeys they took to get to where they are today, which almost always involve commitment, hard work, and a desire to improve their lives. In all the books I read, the authors faced challenges and adversities. Life doesn't throw you a lifeline when you're sitting on the shore. You need to go out into the ocean among the waves and have a go!

Learning from other people's mistakes can fast-track your success. When something doesn't work, or ends in disaster, we automatically learn not to do that thing again. If you touch a hot stove, your brain files away a 'don't touch the hot stove, idiot' command for later reference. It's the same when it comes to business and investing. You learn what works and what doesn't along the way. However, by studying other people's experiences, you can learn that a hot stove will burn you without having to get burnt yourself, to a certain extent. Sure, if you want to find out exactly what touching a hot stove feels like, you can't experience that through a book. However, if you listen and pay attention, you don't have to repeat the same mistakes others have already made.

Tony Robbins has a saying, "Success leaves clues." He believes that by studying successful people, you'll pick up on clues, and I agree. If you study and learn enough about a lot of successful people, you'll start to see patterns, behaviours, and routines that contributed to their success. But you have to be looking for those clues to find them.

I remember reading a Warren Buffet biography and learning about the resistance he faced before he made his wealth. You'd be crazy to question him now, but people genuinely doubted him when he was young. It took years of dedication and applied effort for him to earn his millions, let alone billions, and prove the doubters wrong. *He* knew he was onto something, and he loved what he did with a passion. He lived investing, so it didn't matter what anyone else thought. That's a really important point to remember if you ever go down the entrepreneurial path. People *will* doubt you – it's natural, unavoidable – but if you love what you do and want to create a better life for yourself or your family, you *can* do it. Eventually, you may even get the satisfaction of proving the doubters wrong, or perhaps you'll motivate them to improve their lives too.

WELL, IF HE CAN DO IT...

Let's be real – most of us won't have the opportunity to sit down with Warren Buffet, but most of us *can* pick up his or anyone else's book and learn some valuable stuff. When you read successful people's stories, you realise they're not supernatural beings using magic to gain success – they're human. What happens when you realise that the most successful people in the world are just as human and flawed as the rest of us? You realise that *you* could achieve the same level of success *if* you play the game right. As I mentioned, if you start looking for clues, you'll find them. If you study someone's road to success, you'll see that the clues are everywhere. When they put their life story or life's work into words and package it in a nice, neat manual – that is, a book – cracking the code is even easier. I'm not saying books are the magic solution to success but because I had nothing else to work with, I felt like I'd struck gold. Suddenly, the path to success was all laid out for me.

THAT'S A FACT
Warren Buffet bought his first stock at the fresh age of 11.[12] So, it's never too early – or too late, for that matter – to start investing.

Warren Buffet did it. Why can't I? Steve Jobs did it. Why can't I? Richard Branson did it. Why can't I? If someone has done it, you can do it too. I can do it. The guy down the street can do it. All right, maybe not him. I don't think he's got what it takes. My point is, the opportunities are out there, but they won't come looking for you. It's up to you to find them and grab them by the throat. You won't get far sitting on your couch, playing video games or watching TV. You've got to take action.

For the record, I didn't set out to be the next Warren Buffet. I was enough of a realist to realise I probably wasn't going to make billions. But millions? Well, plenty of people make *millions*, so maybe I could too. When setting goals, it's important to have a healthy mix of ambition *and* realism. Everything should be tied back to your vision and values so you don't deviate from your path. I'm talking about *your* vision, not someone else's. From there, you need clear, measurable goals that you can break down into milestones, with a rough timeline for creating the life you want. Once you have a clear but flexible plan, you can start to take serious action by executing and implementing your ideas.

The one thing I want to stress is to always protect your downside risk because mistakes will happen, and you'll need to make changes to the original plan, which is fine, as long as you don't over-leverage yourself by going all in. When you do finally action everything you've learnt, risk management is super important. It's okay to fail and learn from the experience, but a failure shouldn't result in your ruin.

For me, books were a cheap, easy, and effective way to expand my mind with the wisdom of people who'd already been there, done that. But I couldn't just sit around, wallowing in knowledge forever. Eventually, I had to take action – and I did, immersing myself in the stock market. I was much more knowledgeable than I'd been when I first dabbled in investing, and I now knew the importance of controlling my downside risk. The game was on.

Essentially, I was a bauxite miner by day and a stock trader by night.

THE STOCK MARKET WAS MY PLAYGROUND – FIND YOURS

Because I spent most of my time away from home, working in the mines, I wasn't spending a lot of money. Whenever I was back in Sydney, I'd stay with Mum or Dana. I wasn't earning a massive amount of money, but the pay wasn't terrible, and I practically had no expenses. It was time to put my informal education into action and discover for myself what worked and what didn't. So, based on everything I'd learnt, I started trading shares.

My little mining donga in the desert became a makeshift trading office. I was the only bloke at the mines who didn't have naked girls all over his walls. Instead, I put up stock charts, which included different trading patterns. I was reading books by a lady named Louise Bedford, who explained the 'candlestick formula'. In short, the formula uses trading patterns and investor psychology and movements to try to pinpoint the market direction and, well, make money from it. I also did additional research online, where I read a lot of trading blogs, which were big back then. I set up two computer screens on my tiny desk so I could keep up with everything I was doing. I also installed trading software on my laptop and had internet connected to my room. Sometimes I'd be up most of the night, talking to people in the UK and other countries about trading, with live trades going on in the background. Clearly, I wasn't mucking around. I was deadset serious about mastering the stock market.

Often, I'd be awake at two in the morning, trading in the

UK and European currency markets, implementing day trading strategies with other investors around the world, which sounds quite cool when you think about it. I utilised every resource at my disposal, including forums, online courses – some of which I bought for five to ten grand a pop – and book after book. I was consuming nearly one book per week on average. I was constantly chasing information, but, importantly, I was finally putting it into action. I hungered to become the rich dad (the informally educated dad) from that one book I couldn't forget, and I pursued that path with relentless determination. You can't half-arse these things and expect to win the game.

Whenever any of the other guys in the mine passed by my donga, if the door was open, they'd see walls covered in trading charts and multiple monitors running trading software. I'd even bought furniture that gave the room a corporate office vibe. Of course, they'd laugh at me and say how silly I was to waste my time trading stocks, but I knew better. Most of the people I encountered didn't see the world as I did. They didn't see the same opportunities. Was it all the books I read that shaped my worldview? It definitely helped. All those authors, my unofficial mentors, faced and overcame challenge after challenge on the path to achieving their dreams. Their success inspired me to want more for my life and helped me realise I could be successful too – by whatever definition I chose. I was on my own path, and there was no going back.

Eventually, I turned my attention to property, and I started saving for a deposit on a house. Like I said, I didn't have many expenses, and, growing up the way I did, I was used to living on a tight budget, so putting money aside each week was relatively easy.

The mines provided unlimited buffet-style meals and free access to a decent gym, so I was practically in heaven. At that point, I was the fittest and most focused I'd ever been in my life. With that said, I didn't live like a complete tight-arse. I still went out for beers with my friends and brothers when I was back in Sydney, but I didn't burn money like a lot of young people do. Instead, I put aside a set amount to spend on my weeks back home and didn't spend a cent more. Why? Because I had saving and investment goals to reach. Plus, I felt like I was making up for lost time. I was only 22 years old, but I felt old at the time and was so far behind everyone else in life. Really, I was still a young pup, with no clue about the world or what lay ahead. I didn't understand that what everyone else was doing didn't matter. It was all about me, my goals, and my achievements.

When I decided to get into the property market, I went to the bank and spoke with them to figure out what I needed to do. As a first home buyer, I didn't need a massive deposit, and I soon bought my first house. Finally, I was starting to get ahead in life. The property would increase in value and make money for me while I was away working in the mine, but I knew I had to tread carefully if I wanted to hold on to the small amount of wealth I'd made.

Although I was in the market, my knowledge around property was limited, so I bought a book on Australian investment property tax laws. Yep, it's exactly what it sounds like: line after line of tax laws over hundreds of pages but simplified to be consumable for the average reader. I read that book from front to back, learning how to build a property portfolio in a legal and tax-efficient way.

When trading, one of my main aims – as well as to make money – was to not *lose* money. That's a big one. You've got to play it smart. Breaking even, while not ideal, is fine – just *don't lose money*. It's a simple concept, right? Don't forget it.

Taking big risks may seem like the rockstar entrepreneur move, but it's not the smartest and most effective way to make money. Take Richard Branson, for example. As someone who has achieved extreme levels of wealth and success, you might assume he took some big risks to get there, but that isn't the case. Shocking, right? Let me explain.

When Virgin Atlantic leased its first 747 aircraft from Boeing, Branson struck a deal with the company. If the airline wasn't doing well by the end of the first year of operation, he could hand the aircraft back and cancel the lease. Essentially, he took on zero financial downside risk to secure use of the aircraft he needed to start his airline. By the end of year one, it was clear that people loved Virgin Atlantic, and the company went on to purchase two more aircraft and many more over the years, which was win-win for Branson and Boeing. The deal meant no risk to the rest of Virgin Group but huge potential upside for the airline if it cracked the code of feasibly providing low-cost flights combined with quality customer service.[13]

It's a great example of an entrepreneur in motion – taking on low risk for a potentially high return. You should always cover your downside risk first and consider the upside profits or benefits second. This one lesson saved me a lot of money. Unfortunately, I never learnt it until after I went to the mines, so, as we know,

I lost a lot of money on bad deals. While I had no clue what I was doing, I had the guts to give anything a go to make money, which, in hindsight, was a losing combo. Guts are great but with no real knowledge or experience, I got burnt time and time again. I was so focused on the upside benefits that I didn't consider or attempt to control the risks.

"The first rule of an investment is don't lose. The second rule of an investment is don't forget the first rule. And that's all the rules there are."
– WARREN BUFFET

During this time, I also read a book called *Do It Yourself Developments*. I was nowhere near entering the property development space, but I read the book anyway because it was something I wanted to do in the future. Yeah, I was getting a bit ahead of myself, but I was hungry for knowledge, and I was preparing myself for future goals. I was obsessed with figuring out how other people made their wealth, and property was one of the main vehicles for making millionaires. I've still got that book. Over the years, it has been moved from house to house in box after box, and it's looking pretty weathered, but it's a reminder of where I started my journey into the world of finance, in that cramped mining donga in the desert. I've since got into property development, so reading that book wasn't a complete waste of time. It just took me a while to use the knowledge I acquired. See, long-term goals *and* patience are key.

HOW TO GET BLACKLISTED BY A BUNCH OF BUSINESS BROKERS

As I explored the world of finance, money, and markets, which were all things I was passionate about – who doesn't like money, right? – I also began to explore the business landscape.

You may have noticed a pattern in the opportunities I pursued. Essentially, I was trying to generate passive income by investing, which was one of the cash flow quadrants in *Rich Dad Poor Dad*. In the book, the author explains that there are four ways to create cash flow. The first, which I'd ticked off, is through employment. The second is using employment income to invest and build passive or investment income. This is why I focused so much of my time and attention on the stock market and bought a property. I was trying to create cash flow using the first two methods. The next cash flow option is to become a self-employed specialist, a business owner, who runs their own show and makes good money. However, the drawback to this method is if you stop work for any reason, the cash flow dries up immediately. Finally, the fourth option is to create and grow a business that runs with or without you. That way, the cash flow never stops.[14]

Based on this information, I knew that my next step was to build or run a business, but I had no clue where to start, so, naturally, I chose to learn more. I went to websites that listed businesses for sale and pretended I wanted to buy some of them. Of course, at the time, I could never have bought any of the listings, but I was undercover, gathering information, accumulating knowledge. The problem was, I didn't know what I was talking about. I'd call up and enquire about the business and the financials and whatever else, asking the dumbest questions. I'd then complete the confidentiality agreement (CA) and get the first level of due diligence documents: financials and business overview documents, normally laid out in an information memorandum. I know the lingo now, but back then I was seriously winging it. Looking back, I must have sounded like an absolute dickhead. The brokers I spoke to soon realised I didn't have any money, didn't know what I was talking about, and wasn't buying a business any time soon. They got sick of me really fast, so they blacklisted me, and the game was over. However, I managed to learn a lot of high-level information, including what to ask for, and other critical details and terms, such as net profit, business cash flow, how a business is valued, and what type of finance could be structured to make the deal happen.

The first company I ever set up was called Tycoon Tree, and it still exists to this day. It's the corporate holding company for all my other businesses, but it was originally just a trading company. I didn't even know what a holding company was back then.

Originally, Tycoon Tree was going to be a website where people, after signing up, could find information on property and stock investments, as well as blogs and other resources. They'd also be able to find experts' online courses and services and rate them. Basically, I was creating a social media platform centred around making money. When I got banned from enquiring about businesses, I realised that other people must be out there looking for answers too. So, why not make it easy for them? I'm sure Uncle Keith was also getting pretty sick of me asking questions at every family gathering, and I was probably close to ending up on his own personal blacklist. Although my uncle was highly successful, he wasn't an entrepreneur, and he couldn't teach me everything I wanted to know about business, which was why I needed other sources.

The problem is, sometimes when you're buying an online course or another resource, you don't know if what you're getting has value. Sometimes it's difficult to see through all the marketing and hype. That's why I wanted to build a reputable site where people could exchange ideas and information. If someone was selling a dud course, Tycoon Tree members would quickly know about it.

The flip side to this was letting people know the good deals, services, products, courses, and investments. People could have shared their services while others rated them. Also, members could have collaborated on forums and groups to provide value to each other and the overall online community. What a social platform, right?

Unfortunately, I had no idea what I was doing. At the time, I simply didn't have the knowledge and experience I needed to create something like that. Looking back, it wasn't a bad idea, but I was being too ambitious and not realistic enough, which I eventually realised before abandoning the venture altogether.

I GOT LUCKY WITH MY PASSION

Fortunately for me, I was passionate about finance and business, so my interests were directly related to learning how to make money, which was handy. I was fascinated by the complexity of laws, legislations, and applying them strategically. People at the top seemed to know all the secret rules, the way economics ran the world and connected through the global system, along with the psychology behind being a good investor, and I wanted to learn it all too. Now, I know that not everyone is enthusiastic about the stock market or other big money-making ventures, and we should all do what we're passionate about, whatever that might be. But here's the thing: if your passion isn't going to pay the bills, you need to find another way to generate wealth. Otherwise, you're in for a rough time. Once you do get yourself in a good position financially, then you'll be freer to pursue the things you're passionate about. Whatever you want to do in life, chances are, you still need money.

See, I was more passionate about business and entrepreneurship than I was about finance, but I didn't have the money to go into business, so I played the stock market. Really, it was a stepping stone to where I wanted to go. I also knew I needed a stable income, a stable career, which was why I was content to keep working in the mines until I figured out where to go next.

KNOW THE RULES, PLAY THE GAME, WIN

Regardless of what your goals are in life, you need to learn at least the basics of finances: budgeting, tax, superannuation, and so on. It's a cliché, I know, but money really does make the world go round. It's why I created the True North Academy and my Financial Foundations course – to help people gain an awareness and unbiased view of the tools they have at their disposal. Before you can win the game, you must understand the rules.

If you want to get ahead financially, you need to understand what healthy budgeting looks like. If you've got a job or you're working for yourself, you need to understand the tax system and cash flow to succeed. If you want to fund a certain lifestyle, you need to understand investing and what to do with the money you put aside. Understanding the system we operate within and the tools available is the pathway to financial freedom because when you're weighed down with debt and bills, living a good, fulfilling life isn't easy. I'm not saying it's impossible, but the harsh reality is that most of us need a certain amount of money to be content in this world. It's all about doing what's necessary to provide a better life for you and your family. That doesn't mean money needs to be your main driver, but you shouldn't overlook its usefulness as a tool for freedom.

To drop another cliché – time equals money. But money also equals time. When you hustle hard and hit a certain level of wealth, you start to free up more time to do the things you love. More time with friends and family. More time for holidays. More time to hit the gym. More time for whatever. Maybe you only want to work a 15-hour week and spend the rest of the time pursuing your passions. If so, that's great, but how are you going to fund that? Sure, you could spend those days off just sitting around the house, but most people want to get out, do things, and experience life. To do that, in the conventional sense, you need money in the bank (or stuffed under a mattress). Personally, I wouldn't recommend the mattress. It's a risky move.

Anyway, I'm not saying you have to take the path I took, staying up until 2 am trading stocks. You might even be able to turn *your* passion into a profitable venture. Ask yourself, is there a market for what you want to offer or create? If so, that may very well be the path of least resistance to making good money.

Whether you end up as an employee or a business owner, you're going to need at least a basic level of financial knowledge if you want to get the most out of your situation. The more you know, the better. Once you do learn enough to be dangerous – I mean that in a positive way – you're ready to determine the road you'll take to the life you imagine. What do you want? Freedom? Wealth? Time? Something else? What must you do to get there?

Once you have a good overview of your options, you need to articulate your vision, know your values, who you want to become, and the steps needed to make your ideal life a reality. This means setting measurable goals. Backed by the knowledge of how to get to where you want to go, you can then start taking action, implementing what you've learnt, and even enjoying the process. Don't forget the importance of celebrating the small wins along the way. You will face setbacks, which you'll need to reflect on. You should embrace and reflect on the wins too.

If you do decide to go down an unconventional path or one you're outwardly unsuited for, like I eventually did, you're going to meet a whole lot of doubters along the way. Fuck them. If I'd listened to all those naysayers, I wouldn't have done a fraction of what I did, and I wouldn't be where I am today. I've built businesses, performed mergers and acquisitions, handled insanely high levels of cash flow, and, in one of my businesses, I'm responsible for investing nearly half a billion dollars of clients' funds under management – it still blows my mind. When I first pinned those trading charts up on my wall, I couldn't have dreamed I'd be where I am today. I still lacked self-belief, and having person after person question what I was doing didn't help. Fear and doubt can be dangerous if you let them creep in. But I persevered, and hopefully I inspired at least some of the doubters to find their own paths to success.

My fuel was the drive to prove that I could do it. The thing is, if I can do it, so can you. You don't need to accept the status quo, the same day in, day out routine, with no progress or growth moving you closer to the life you want. Part of what I want to do now is help others understand they have limitless potential. We let our upbringings, our environments, our conditioning, and the people around us limit us, but those limitations aren't real. They're just in our heads. We can either be slaves to those false limitations, or we can shed the mental shackles and start making things happen.

What do you want your life to look like ten years from now? Remember, long-term thinking is vital, especially if things aren't going so well right now. Maybe you're broke. Maybe you don't have a career or profitable business. None of that matters. Again, what do you want your life to look like ten years from now? Where do you want to be? What does life on your terms look like? Seriously, think about it. Whatever you imagine, you may not believe it, but if you're being realistic, it *is* impossible.

I've found that most people don't want extravagant lives. They don't want to be Bill Gates or Jeff Bezos or Mark Zuckerberg. Of course, you get the crazy ones who think they can reach that level of success, but they usually haven't given it a lot of thought and don't understand how much work is involved. What I'm saying is, most people I speak to have realistic goals, like less work, more holidays, early retirement, really achievable stuff. They're not asking for a mansion in Dover Heights or a solid gold toilet, although it would be nice. The mansion, I mean. Not sure what I'd do with the toilet.

Once you get control of your money and understand how the system works, most down-to-earth dreams are achievable.

Knowledge is critical, but confidence is also a big factor. When you feel like you're in control, you get better at pulling the right levers to get the outcomes you want.

I know that in a world where it's getting harder and harder to get ahead financially, especially for the younger generations, making short-term sacrifices for long-term gain doesn't seem as worth it as it once did. To many, saving up for a house deposit seems like an impossible goal, so they spend their money on overseas holidays, experiences, and, as some would claim, smashed avo on toast. Why would you sacrifice your quality of life now for a goal that seems impossible? You wouldn't, right? That's why we first need to understand our potential – our real potential, not what others tell us we're capable of – so we know what *is* possible. Remember, potential is practically limitless. Granted, life, if you look at it as a race to success, is far from fair. We don't all have the same training or equipment, and we don't all start from the same position. Quite frankly, the race is rigged, but that doesn't mean the underdog can't win. In fact, as you'll soon learn, often the underdogs are the most determined to succeed.

WAS I EVER GOING TO BE GOOD ENOUGH?

When I was in the mines, about two years into my three-and-a-half-year stint as a miner, I began formally studying financial planning, not because I wanted to be a financial planner but because I wanted to learn more about controlling my finances, as my income had increased exponentially.

As is often the case with hard work and commitment, the higher ups noticed me, and, after several new roles and promotions,

I landed a job in a gold mine in Orange as a leading hand. I was taking home over $3,500 in my hand each week. To earn that money, I'd work six days a week and get every Sunday off. Also, while I was there, I bought another house and renovated it from top to bottom.

Although I was on a good wicket, I refused to settle. I was still stuck in a less than ideal situation, trading six days per week, 12 hours per day for all that money. I needed an exit plan. From my investments, I was getting really good returns, and I wanted to become better at investing and managing my finances. Finally, I felt confident in my abilities and felt that I could complete some formal education, which was what led to me studying financial planning. One way or another, I was always on the path of learning.

When I began studying, the other guys at the mine would see what I was doing, with all the textbooks piled up and trading charts on the walls, and, naturally, they laughed and gave me shit for it. But they were just a few more people in a long line of doubters who couldn't wait to tell me I was wasting my time. Sometimes you've just got to tune out the noise and keep pushing forward.

While I didn't know what to do next, I knew I couldn't stay in the mines. I saw what a career in mining did to people. Like I said, many of the blokes ahead of me in years and experience were divorced or had broken families. They were alcoholics and compulsive gamblers. Ultimately, over years, their relationships fell apart, and they coped by drinking and gambling all their money away. I'd experienced what working away does to a relationship, and I knew I couldn't do it long-term. I needed a way out, and financial planning seemed like something I could do.

If I could complete my qualification, it would open up a new pathway for me. But how would I, of all people, become a financial planner? Was this something I could actually see myself doing? I was, after all, a high school dropout with a delinquent past. But my new way of thinking kicked in, and I realised I was more than capable. I'd been investing successfully for some time, and my net wealth was taking off. Clearly, I already knew a thing or two about managing money. I also knew a lot of the terminology and different tax rules and legislations that only the rich were using. I felt that I had already achieved what I once thought impossible. So, why not aim higher? I'd be silly to not even try.

The goal was to challenge my potential… but where to start? *I know! Uncle Keith will get me a job.* Great idea, right? So, yeah, I was wrong on that front. Although we got on great and he gave me plenty of advice, he struggled to see past the shitbag kid with a troubled past and a history of making stupid decisions. There was no way Uncle Keith was going to stake his good name on me. Why would he? He's a smart man. He knows a risky gamble when he sees one. So, if I wanted a job, I'd need to get it myself. How hard could it be? I had a diploma in financial planning, so I was qualified, right? I'd already done the hard part, applying myself to gaining my qualification and passing with a distinction for all subjects, right? *Right?* As it turned out, it wasn't that simple.

I put in countless applications and never got an interview. Now, at this point in my life, I was pretty extroverted, so I didn't hesitate to call up and find out why I was being overlooked, explaining how much I knew and what I'd done to get to where I was. Every conversation went something like this: "Look, Kane, I'll be honest with you. Forty people applied for this job, and pretty much all of them had university degrees. Of those forty, at least half of them had a master's in finance. So, I just took those top candidates, the ones with master's degrees, picked the best of the lot, and called them in for interviews. That way, we get a good candidate with all the qualifications."

That stung. Not only did I not get an interview, but, due to my lack of high-level, formal education, I wasn't even a consideration. The thing is, we know now that IQ and education aren't the biggest indicators of success. How many talented people get overlooked in the job market because they don't have the formal qualifications? Now, I'm not saying I was particularly talented compared to the other candidates, but I felt like I had more practical knowledge and skills. I'd been running teams in mining projects, trading in the share markets, and acquiring multiple properties. In my mind, if they'd just allow me one interview, they'd see what I had to offer. The problem was, I hadn't proven myself by obtaining higher education or years of industry experience, so, on paper, I wasn't an appealing candidate. Even so, I thought I'd at least get a look-in. Yeah, I should've known better. The job market can be brutal, especially when it comes to highly skilled positions. So, what could I do?

I didn't have the credentials or experience to impress the recruiters, and Uncle Keith still saw me as the troubled kid who got kicked out of school and couldn't hold a job. But I'd grown a lot since then. Why couldn't anyone see it? I'd come this far on my own, and I wasn't about to start letting the doubters hold me back now.

I sat down one day after letting the self-doubt dominate my thoughts, creating stories and letting myself feel like I should've listened to the doubters. *Everyone was right. Working in the mines was the best way to get ahead.* But I couldn't let those thoughts consume me. Instead, I needed to reset, remind myself why I started this journey, and reflect on how far I'd already come, overcoming multiple struggles along the way. So, I went back to my vision and imagined the future Kane, my future family, and what they would say to me, what they would think. I realised I had no excuses for giving up. I still had a driving purpose behind my why, and I wasn't ready to settle, not yet. I'd barely touched the surface of the life I wanted to create. I'd force my way into the world of finance, one way or another. Yep, I wasn't giving up so easily – not a chance! So, it was back to the drawing board for a new strategy to break into the world of finance.

BIGGEST INSIGHTS FROM THE FOURTH CHAPTER OF MY LIFE

Just start – Sometimes you just need to start, even if you don't know exactly what you want to do or what you want your life to look like. It's like going to a restaurant and not knowing what you want from the menu. If you don't order something and taste a few different foods, you'll never know what you like. So, go out there, and try different things until you know what you want to do and where you want to go. It will be an exciting experience and a rewarding part of your journey. Ultimately, doing something is much better than doing nothing.

Protect your downside risk – When it comes to making money, the smartest investors, like Richard Branson, know to protect their downside risk. Capping or controlling the risk in a business venture or investment is key and should be understood right from the start. Next, you can focus on potential for return, assessing the situation diligently and without emotion. I've seen way too many investors and business owners learn these lessons the hard way. The lives of others, their successes and their failures, can teach us a lot. When it came to trading shares, I learnt a lot from online communities, forums, blogs, and meet-ups, which, together, provided a world of information. Remember, I spent most of my spare time in a small cabin in a mining camp. I had to find help wherever I could, so I turned to the internet. Wherever you are, find a good community to help you learn the valuable lessons and skills you'll need to reach your goals.

Find your passion – If your passion doesn't involve money and finances, you don't have to be an investor. Instead, you might find a hobby you love that can become a business. Or if your hobby isn't something you can turn into a business, or you don't want to mix work and play, you can still learn about money and upskill yourself to create a life where you have more time to focus on your hobbies, or your family. In my case, the investment world, chasing businesses, and entrepreneurship were in my blood – I couldn't deny it. So, I pursued entrepreneurship and a business in finance, where I now work on strategies and invest-ment solutions for others. It's my passion, and I make a good living, providing for my family and living the life I want. You don't have to follow the same path. Just do whatever works for you.

Never stop learning – Knowledge is key to any outcome. On your journey to the life you desire, good, practical knowledge and skills will help you improve your health, your wealth, and your life in general. Never give up the pursuit of knowledge. Always seek learning and growth.

Prepare for the struggle – On your journey to success, you *will* experience struggle, and self-doubt can show its ugly head. When the doubt does creep in, you need to remember why you started this journey in the first place. Being clear on your why, your vision, and your purpose will help you overcome any self-doubt that arises. Setbacks can, and likely will, occur. Mistakes will be made. As I said, you need to protect your downside risk so the setbacks aren't catastrophic. Smart, diligent steps are key. With good knowledge and a supportive community behind you, you'll have the best chance of reaching your goals. When the voice of self-doubt does creep in, your vision, your purpose, and your why have the power to silence it.

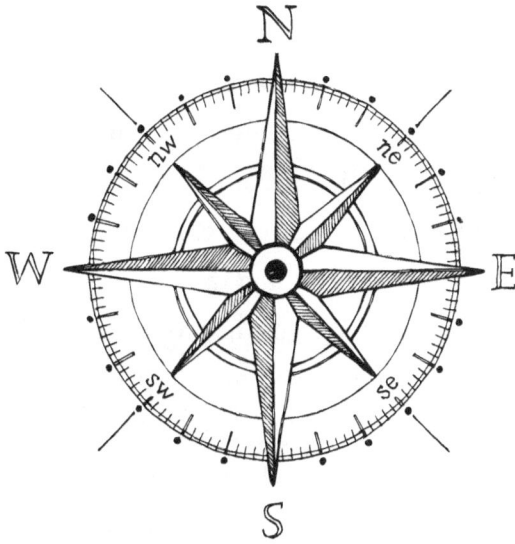

CHAPTER 5

CHARGING INTO THE WORLD OF FINANCE

IS THAT AN OPENING I SEE?

Aside from my diploma in financial planning, which, as we know, didn't stack up against a university degree, I didn't have anything shiny to wave in front of recruiters. Technically, I did have all the self-education I'd put myself through in the mines, but, to a busy recruiter, that didn't mean shit. If I couldn't get a job in the industry through the typical channels, I needed to find another way in. Finally, the ideal solution presented itself.

At the time, AMP was running the Career Changer Program, which was similar to an internship program. As the name suggests, the program was designed to help people shift into careers as financial planners – exactly what I wanted to do. So far so good. They also weren't fussy about who could apply, as long as they showed potential and had the minimum qualifications to meet the ASIC requirements to be a financial planner. Basically, it was an internship designed for someone exactly like me. *Where do I sign up?*

While it wasn't a massive program, I was still up against hundreds of applicants for a spot in the top 30 or so they accepted with every intake. First, I had to apply online and try to stand out among the hundreds of other applicants across Australia. If I was successful, I'd need to attend a half-day, onsite event at one of their corporate training buildings to complete an initial skills test. The test would include questions about financial markets, maths related to investments and finance, and a section on tax. Essentially, it was designed to ensure candidates had the basic knowledge needed for the role. Thankfully, I was good at maths and had read so many finance books over the years that I knew my stuff, and I had no trouble passing the test. So, my résumé would get looked at. But would the recruiters like what they saw? Yeah, my mining background wasn't going to impress them, so hopefully something else would.

Somehow, I caught their attention because I scored an interview. Honestly, they probably just wanted to meet the ex-miner who thought he could do finance, but a way in is a way in. I wasn't complaining. I did manage to ace a few sections of the exam, so that probably had something to do with it too. In the first round of interviews, they mentioned that I got 100 percent in the tax skills section, which was practically unheard of, as that knowledge isn't generally at the core of a finance degree. It's more practical knowledge for people in financial planning roles. With solid maths skills and all the tax knowledge I'd gained from books and implemented in life, along with the experience of managing several investments, I had an advantage, or a foot in the door at the very least.

Now, as a self-taught extrovert, a people person, someone who loves a good chat, interviews are where I shine. However, I had to deal with the shock of finding out at the first interview that every other person who'd made it that far had a university degree, some with double degrees, masters of finance, and others not directly related to finance. But I had something they didn't: experience in the real world – street smarts. I wasn't coming in with soft hands and stars in my eyes. I had to hone in on my strengths, put my best foot forward, and show them what I could do differently. I had to demonstrate the things I knew and the skills I had that other candidates lacked. In life, you have to play to your strengths and create every advantage you can. I couldn't wow them with a degree I didn't have, and I doubt they'd be impressed if I told them I'd dropped out of high school, so I needed to show them why I deserved to be in the program.

The interview mainly focused on how I managed to achieve such high marks in the test, especially in the tax section. I was, after all, just a young man with a mining background and no higher education degree under my belt. I completed three interviews in total, doing particularly well in the final interview, which was based around role-playing scenarios. While I did have a wealth of knowledge, much of it self-learned, my communication skills were my real strength. Once they saw I wasn't the biggest bogan in the world – come on, I was fairly presentable for an ex-miner – they were seriously considering me for a spot in the program. Eventually, they whittled the applicant pool down from hundreds of candidates to 30 new interns, and I was one of them. Finally, I'd found an opening into the world of finance, and I'd be charging in headfirst.

When they offered me the job, they told me I was the only intern with no degree. I was the only person from a blue-collar background who got through the interviews and the onboarding process. They definitely let me know there was a lot weighing on my success, and everyone would be watching to see how I performed.

FROM HIGH SCHOOL DROPOUT TO TOP STUDENT

Once I got accepted into the Career Changer Program, I was in for an intense 12-week training program, just like in the *Pursuit of Happyness*. If you've seen the movie, you'll know what I'm talking about. It was 100 percent like the internship in the movie, which the main character, played by Will Smith, went through. If you don't know the movie, go watch it. It's based on an amazing true story and is a great watch overall.

The textbooks were *thick*, and we had to sit and pass an exam every two weeks before they'd put us in a live financial planning environment. For five days a week, we were in the classroom, and the expectations were brutal. The pass mark for the exams was 80 percent, with a final collective test at the end of the 12 weeks. Although they showed a little leniency in the fortnightly exams, if I didn't achieve at least 80 percent in the final test, I'd be out of the program. Was I going to let that rattle me? Fuck no. It just motivated me to work harder.

Every day, I sat at the front of the class – by choice this time, unlike my high school days – and asked question after question. Yeah, I was *that* guy, the one who doesn't shut up and won't stop asking questions, but I was simply doing what was necessary. See, I'm a kinesthetic learner, which means I need to interact to learn. But once I learn something, I never forget it. I retain a lot of weird information, but sometimes it comes in handy. The other interns even tried to pull me up on my constant questioning, asking why I had to ask so many questions right before lunch or knock-off time, as they wanted to get out early. I didn't understand why they *weren't* asking questions. Maybe they were used to learning at a high volume. Or perhaps they felt more confident in their abilities or already knew the material. Either way, it didn't matter to me. I only needed to focus on myself.

I knew that, because of my lack of formal education, getting ahead would be harder for me. To succeed, I'd need to be attentive, engaged, and maximise my time with the teacher. After so many failed job applications, I wasn't going to waste the opportunity. No, I'd make the most of it and ask as many questions as necessary to understand the material, even if it pissed the other students off.

By the end of the 12-week program, I was among the top students in the class. My hard work and dedication paid off, but the real work was about to begin. After training, whoever survived now had to apply all the theory they'd learnt and prove themselves in the real world.

THE BATTLE BEGINS

Once I passed all the exams, I was thrown into an advisory environment and given a list of 200 of the lowest-value potential clients, with the smallest balances or policies, they could scrape from the bottom of the barrel. I'm talking people who had almost no money to their names, at least not with the bank I was operating under. Most of them didn't even know their accounts or policies existed, and they certainly didn't want to talk to someone like me, someone they thought was just trying to sell them more crap from a call centre.

From here, the program consisted of nine months in the live advisory environment where we had to convert our own clients. The target was over 20 clients signed up and fully advised throughout the remainder of the program. Challenge accepted. It was game time, and there was no looking back.

Some interns didn't have the soft skills to convert people in the database, so they resorted to signing up family members. We were allowed to use people in our own personal networks, but jeez… I couldn't imagine trying to persuade my own parents or family to sign up just to get my numbers up. Each to their own, I suppose. It's a dog-eat-dog world – that's for sure. If someone signed up their mum and dad separately, well, that's two new sign ups. That's how some people got their numbers up, but, even if I wanted to go down that path, I didn't have a big family network to draw on, or family that had the money to spare even if they felt that I could deliver a good result, so I had to do it the hard way.

I hit the phones hard, trying to spark even a hint of interest in what I was offering. But converting people to clients was only half the battle. Once I'd signed someone up, I actually had to fix their finances, all while meeting compliance requirements and other KPIs (key performance indicators). At the end of the nine months, not everyone was guaranteed a job, so the pressure was on.

I spent most days, and many nights, cold calling people about lost super, but I had to be smart about how I communicated with them. If I opened with the wrong line, many would swiftly tell me to "fuck off," or the polite ones would just hang up. So, I developed a script that would pique people's interest instead of pissing them off.

If I said 'super fund', I'd lose them immediately. They hated the word. So, instead, I'd say something like, "Hey, my name's Kane, sorry to bother you, but there's an account here with money in it and your name on it. Would you have a minute to chat about it?"

Who wouldn't be interested in an account they own with money in it? The key was to tell them who I was and how I could help them within the first 20 seconds of the call. If I could convince them I was legit and that I could actually do something for them, they'd be willing to talk to me. Ultimately, people just want to know, "What's in it for me?"

To improve my game, I found a free calling script online, created by another successful financial adviser in New Zealand. He had a process for building rapport and trust with clients and taking a cold lead who's not interested in talking to you and turning them around. The key is to show them you're there to help and explain how you can fix their problem with a fast solution. I'm not telling you this to help you sell more or build rapport, although it is an important communication skill. The underlying lesson here is: even if you don't have the right skills, or you're stuck, the solution is out there. There's an immense amount of information available to help you learn faster and more efficiently. Whatever your goals or dreams are, you *can* gain the knowledge you need to achieve them, if you're willing to work and not give up.

When I was trying to convert clients, if I did manage to persuade someone to meet with me, I'd often end up driving out to places like Western Sydney, rocking up at 9 pm in the little yellow car my missus owned because I was low on cash, and it was good on fuel. I'd exit the car, wondering if I was mad to even be there, knock, introduce myself, and enter the house, which was usually cluttered with useless junk, not to mention the five or so cats, and then I'd desperately try to sign the person up. If I wanted a job at the end of my internship, I had to perform. Often, I'd leave at 10:30 pm without signing them up because they didn't understand what I was saying. No matter how I explained it, they just didn't get what was going on. But I didn't have a choice. If I wanted to hit my targets, I had to put in the effort and the hours. I was constantly pursuing greatness and continuing to improve my call script, my meeting agenda, and the methods I used to explain the services I was offering.

During the internship, we did get paid, but, compared to what I'd earned in the mines, it wasn't much. By the time I left the mines, I'd worked my way up to foreman, and, as you know, I was on pretty good money. Leaving that role was madness. I'd worked my way up and achieved close to a top-level mining income, and to hit the reset button and start a new career, beginning again at the bottom and learning everything from scratch, didn't make sense. So, when I took the internship, I essentially took an 80 percent pay cut. At the time, I had two mortgages, and my partner didn't contribute much. Really, she did little more than rack up huge credit card bills. While she was an amazing, supportive partner, budgeting definitely wasn't her strength. Funnily enough, that relationship didn't work out.

During the program, most weeks, I got down to my last $80, which was surplus income I could spend on leisure items like eating out, seeing a movie, or just getting a takeaway pizza. I barely had any disposable income and got used to being broke again. Of course, I still had a decent little share portfolio from when I was moonlighting as a stock trader, so, over time, I sold most of it off to keep me afloat. Over the course of the 12-month program, to manage the costs of my rental properties, especially if a tenant left at the end of a lease or a repair was needed, or if I wanted a long weekend away, the shares were there to use as capital. All I had to do was survive long enough to get to the other end of the program.

The thing is, when I accepted the internship, I was willing to take the financial hit. I didn't see it as a step backwards, quite the opposite, in fact. Long term, I knew that I was making a good decision and the sacrifices would be worth it in the end. I grew up poor, remember? If I had to go back to eating Mum's beef mince recipes, so be it. Eventually, I'd be back to earning big money like I did in the mines – at least, that was my goal.

With a good serving of hard work and a side of perseverance, I was able to keep up with the other interns and surpass some of them. The thing is, once you start to win, people begin to turn on you. They talk shit behind your back. They try to bring you down. Not everyone reacts this way to someone else's success, but there's usually at least a few in every group. The ones who talked shit – guess what? They weren't the high performers. Do you know why? Because they were too busy focusing on what everyone else was doing, neglecting their own performance. When they were failing, they made excuses, but I grew up in an environment where excuses were worthless, so I ignored the noise and kept my eye on the prize.

Remember, I was the one with no degree and no large personal network of people to sign up, so I had to work hard for every inch of success. Some of the most highly educated candidates, with the most family members signed up, were starting to point fingers, questioning why I was doing so well. They said I must be cutting corners, lying, or cheating. But do you know what? It just made me hungrier. I kept my head down and my nose clean, focusing only on what was ahead. For me, there was no looking back. The more I achieved, the more my confidence grew, and the loftier my goals became.

The whole experience made me realise how important it is to focus only on what you're doing. Don't pay attention to others – it's a waste of time and energy. Who cares what the person next to you is up to? Don't look at where *they* are. Instead, look at where *you're* going. If you're looking sideways, you're not looking forward. Do you want to go sideways or forward? If you want to go forward, that's where you need to look.

We live in a world of comparison, with social media at its highest level of usage ever, which makes sense. It is, after all, only a fairly new phenomenon. We spend a lot of time online, comparing our lives, financial positions, and relationships to others – people we don't even know. This is insane. The best action you can take is to block it all out and focus on your own journey, your own progress and goals. If you can't mentally block people out, then either unfollow them or physically block them. I'm not just talking about celebrities and influencers either. The same goes for your friends and close circle of influence. If you do use social media, you can get a lot of value from following inspirational people who motivate you. As long as you're a better person tomorrow than you were today, you're winning.

Others in the program grew resentful because I was an uneducated ex-miner. I couldn't spell, but I was one of the top-performing interns. I was leading in conversion rate, revenue, and number of clients, as I'd managed to get a few quality clients out of the seemingly shitty ones from the database. Some of them had money in other places and when I demonstrated my value and showed I could help solve a problem for them, they were happy to work with me. Before I knew it, I'd discovered the formula for succeeding as a financial adviser. I built trust with my clients, provided value, and, importantly, got results.

So, about the spelling... When I said I couldn't spell, I meant I *really* couldn't spell. I once sent out a group email about something urgent I wanted to share with the team. Even though we were all competing, I did collaborate and exchange ideas with a few of the others I got along with in the program. So, how did I alert everyone to the urgency of my email? I wrote ERGENT in the subject line. I had no idea what I'd done until my mate, Luke, came over and told me.

"Hey, man, about that last email... You need to spellcheck your emails before you send them out. You spelled it wrong."

"Spellcheck? Spelled what wrong?"

"Urgent. It's *U*-R-G-E-N-T." Before joining the Career Changer Program, Luke was a physiotherapist, a highly educated guy, so he'd know. He was from the Northern Beaches, and we got along well. His intentions were always good, so I trusted him.

"Shit."

Clearly, I had my shortcomings, but I wasn't going to let terrible spelling, or anything else, hold me back. I knew the program was a golden opportunity for someone like me. If I didn't finish at the front of the pack, I'd miss out on the good jobs, or I might not get a job offer at all. I was hungry because, unlike many of the other interns, I didn't have qualifications or another career to fall back on, unless I wanted to go back to the mines, which wasn't an option. No, I saw something better for myself.

From day one of the program, I knew I needed to maximise my time and become one of the top performers. The top interns always walked away with the best jobs, fast-tracking their careers.

I wanted to get picked up by a large, successful practice, not some small, one-planner business with average wealth clients, where I'd only be doing middle-class strategies. My plan was to leverage the outcome of the program to take the best first step possible in my new career. Big practice, great mentor, high-net-worth clients – that was the goal. It wasn't just about the money, either. With wealthier clients, the advice and strategies would be more complex, making for a better learning experience. I wanted to learn from the best.

As I grew more confident in my abilities as a financial adviser, I saw myself working in a prestigious office somewhere, wearing a suit and tie – you know, like a respectable sort of bloke. It was someone I never thought I'd be. It was a place I never thought I'd get to. But, day by day, my vision was becoming a reality.

WHEN THE SHARK STARTS CIRCLING...

Working in the live adviser environment, I kept pushing myself to perform. I'm not saying others weren't working hard, but I'm sure I needed it more. Did I want to end up back in the mines? Hell no. For me, failure wasn't an option. So, I was putting in the extra hours and really pushing myself.

Some days, I'd be going through the admin work with my coach, and I'd be seriously struggling. Yeah, I struggled with that stuff, especially with Excel spreadsheets. I'd spent years on the tools, and I didn't understand spreadsheet software. I didn't understand Excel at all, so I just worked everything out on a calculator and typed the numbers in manually. Every day, I spent so many extra hours getting the same output as everyone else who did know how to use Excel. It was a fucking nightmare. I had so much emotion bottled up that, some days, I felt like crying. I was so close yet so far. I was there, but I wasn't. I'd made it, but I hadn't. I was working insane hours, barely earning enough to stay afloat, and I didn't even know if I'd land a job at the end. Some days, I felt like I was on top of the world, getting good results and proving I could do the job. Other days, I didn't feel like I knew what I was doing at all. I didn't know the next step forward. For example, although I was good with strategy and numbers, I struggled with writing and structuring complex documents. On those days, I was on struggle street to say the least, and the lows kicked in.

Don't get me wrong – on the road to success, you'll want to quit. You'll feel like a failure. You'll doubt yourself. You'll doubt everything you're doing. You might even cry. Yes, you'll have bad days, but you'll also have good days where you learn, grow, and get results. It's important to celebrate even the small wins because they'll help when times get tough. The path of an entrepreneur can be rough and lonely. It's not all fun and excitement, but commitment to the lifestyle gets us through to the other side, where the real fun begins. Just remember to enjoy the ride, embrace the journey, because one day it will end, and you'll wish you'd enjoyed yourself more and perhaps taken yourself a little less seriously.

Some days, the vision I had for myself, the successful financial adviser, making 250-plus grand a year, was difficult to see. With my previous experience and qualifications, I could have walked into a mine that day and made similar money. It was dangerous thinking that could have derailed my new career before it had even begun, but we all have doubts. If I made it through

– and I *would* make it through – I'd be in an office somewhere, wearing a suit and tie, helping people with their finances, and, importantly, doing what I loved. Eventually, I'd be back on good money, and I'd never go without again. It'd be five-star beef mince for me then!

Sometimes some of the big dogs in the financial world would come into the office to give talks to the interns. One of those people was a guy named Russell, who would often come in just to inspect the new talent. See, Russell was a thinker, and he knew the value of getting familiar with the top performers before the program ended. He was a top performer himself, as was his practice. We had a scoreboard up in the office, which outsiders weren't meant to see, but Russell would sneak into that section when visiting and look to see who he was going to poach. Naturally, he only wanted the best, as that was the standard he set for his practice and clients.

Russ – he hated it when I called him that – had one of the fastest-growing practices within our financial planning industry network, so getting poached by him would be a great career starter for anyone in the program. He wanted to scale his company by bringing on advisers who'd eventually become partners with him and run some of his businesses. Towards the end of the nine-month program, I was ranking number one, with one other guy, Scotty, close behind, which obviously caught Russ's attention.

One day, I got a random phone call. It was Russell. He'd come in and given a talk a few weeks earlier, so I knew who he was. He convinced me I should meet with him in the training area, off the record, next time he visited. A few days later, he sat me down in one of the meeting rooms, one with a big whiteboard, and started asking questions.

"What's your background, work experience, education?" he asked.

"I used to be a miner," I said, "working in bauxite and gold mines." I explained how I had no degree, mentioned the pathway I took to get into the program, along with the personal investments and trading I'd done.

"And you're number one in the program?"

"Yeah."

"How?"

"Look, I'm still struggling in some areas, but I'm getting better. Right now, I'm just working hard and learning what I can."

He paused in thought. "I want you to come and work for me. With your ability, managing to rank number one in the program with only limited training and knowledge, not to mention your mining background, I can see you've got potential." He grabbed a marker and started excitedly writing on the board, explaining his vision and the future he saw for me. "In two years' time," he said, "we'll buy a million-dollar business, which you'll run under me as a joint venture partnership. Once I've mentored you and you're ready, of course." He ran me through the numbers and explained the process. "This is how I built my $8-million company – by buying other business, doing acquisitions." Today, his company is likely worth over $15 million, and he lives in a $12 million waterfront mansion. "I'll teach you everything I know, and in two years you'll be running and growing a million-dollar business with me. How does that sound?"

"Two years? That's too long."

"Man, you kids, always so eager. You've still got a lot to learn." He paused. "But if you've managed to come this far in such a short time, you've obviously got something. Look, running a business is a whole new game, but within two years I can mould you into someone who really knows what he's doing. I'll fast-track your education in finance and business as much as possible, but you can't take any shortcuts. Shortcuts don't work. To succeed at this stuff, you have to know what you're doing. So, what do you say?"

Some of the coaches in the program had warned us about Russ. They said he was ruthless, aggressive in his tactics, and would do whatever it took to get to the top. If someone didn't perform, he let them go, with zero notice or remorse. It didn't matter if they'd been with the company for six months or six years. If they slipped and didn't hit their targets or meet his high standards, they were out the door. Yeah, the man was ruthless, but you can't say he didn't get results, so, naturally, I accepted his offer and went to work for Russ as a junior adviser.

Finally, I'd completed my internship and was on my way to the life I wanted to create. I'd be an entrepreneur, working in the finance space, with Russ as my mentor, helping people manage their money and achieve *their* goals. What a career! What a life! Everything was falling into place.

MY BIG GAMBLE

Russ was a super smart guy. Before he went out on his own, he was a fund manager under one of the best economists in the country. In his mid 40s, Russ left the fund manager space to pursue a career as a financial planner. Due to his knowledge of the strategies fund managers use to acquire assets and his under-standing of modelling numbers and cash flow forecasting, he had a notable edge. With his knowledge and a bit of hard work, he was able to scale his business fast. How did he do this? Instead of relying on traditional methods, such as word of mouth or net-working, to get clients and grow his business, he acquired other financial planning practices, becoming a multimillionaire in just a few years. Strategic acquisitions were the key.

Clearly, Russ was intelligent, driven, and successful, but my coaches were right – he was a difficult person to be around. He treated people like numbers and was determined to win at all costs. Winning is great, of course, but my values hadn't changed – I never forgot my past – and Russ and I clashed on many occasions.

Being the top intern, I could've interviewed for jobs at other practices, which was what my coaches were pushing for, but Russ was very persuasive. He got in my ear and tried to turn me to the dark side. Who wouldn't want to partner in a million-dol-lar business opportunity at 25 years old? Honestly, most people would struggle to turn down an offer like that. Because I was so ambitious and unwilling to waste a single opportunity, I dove in wholeheartedly.

So, was Russ full of shit, or would I really be running a mil-lion-dollar business in a couple of years? Well, he was right and wrong. He was right about buying a financial planning business within the two-year timeframe, almost to the day. But he was wrong about one thing. We didn't buy a million-dollar business; we bought a *$2-million* business, which I was set to run. Let's backtrack a bit.

When I started working with Russ, he put me on as an associate adviser under him. The guy did back-to-back meetings
every week, which associates rotated in and out of. So, almost
every day, I'd sit in on three or four of those meetings and see
Russ in action. I was constantly absorbing technical information
and advice, taking every opportunity to expand my knowledge.
Also, Russ didn't handle simple clients with low finances like I
was used to dealing with as an intern at the bank. After eight
years of scaling his business, he had approximately 12 staff and
was managing around $500 million of funds, which is a huge
amount to gain in such a short period. As an associate, the plan
was for me to learn from him as fast as I could and mirror his
approach. I'll admit, the first few months were really difficult. I
felt like I was in over my head, but, gradually, I started to get it.
By the six-month mark, I was hungry for more.

"I want you to put me on as an adviser," I said. "I'm ready."

"What makes you think you're ready?"

"I was an adviser previously at the bank, and I've learnt a lot
since then. As you know, I've conducted the entire process now
for over two hundred clients."

"Let me think about it."

Russ hesitated for a couple of weeks, but I persisted, until one
day… "Okay, I'll give you the opportunity… but if I put you on as
an adviser and you fall under the KPIs, you're out. Deal?"

Russ was ruthless like that. While he wasn't shy about letting
us prove ourselves, there was always a catch. If we bit something
off, we had to be damn sure we could chew it; otherwise, we were
out the door.

At the time, I was arrogant, ignorant, and overambitious. With that said, it's not like I didn't assess the risks. I knew there was a chance I would stuff it up and wasn't as ready as I thought I was, but I also knew I could get a job at another practice if Russ gave me the boot. So, I accepted the challenge and put my job on the line.

Russ sat in on a few meetings, and he seemed impressed.

"That was one of the better meetings I've seen in a while." Not exactly super high praise, but, for Russ, it was as good as it got, so I took it.

After I surpassed everyone's expectations, including my own, he let me run loose. A year and a half later, we started looking at businesses, and, eventually, the right one popped up, with a $2-million price tag. Now, you don't just buy a business like that on a whim. I won't go into detail about what's involved in buying a multimillion-dollar business, but it wasn't something that happened overnight. It was a complicated process.

At the end of the day, Russ not only fulfilled his promise, but he overdelivered, and I was on the fast track to the wealth and success I'd dreamed of.

When we were in the process of buying the first business, I knew I wanted more. By this time, Russ was in his mid-50s, and I was a hungry 27-year-old full of ambition. Eventually, he'd retire, and he'd need someone to take over the main business. So, I negotiated with him to ensure that person would be me. When Russ finally did transition to retirement, I'd have first rights to his main business, which would mean a life and future I couldn't have ever imagined.

It was all laid out, the deal signed and sealed. All I had to do now was turn up to work and continue to follow the process, and I'd be first in line to acquire Russ's main business. Simple, right?

STREET SMARTS VS. BOOK SMARTS

In the real world, being book smart only gets you so far. You've also got to be street smart. You could have the best education imaginable but if you don't have common sense, awareness, and social skills, you're going to get left behind.

It's the one thing I had going for me when I jumped into the world of finance: I was street smart. I didn't have a fancy degree, but I did know how to navigate social situations. I knew how to interact with people to get favourable outcomes.

If I hadn't experienced the environment I grew up in, there was no way I would've had the success I did in the internship, cold calling people who wanted nothing to do with me and persuading them to sign up as clients. Looking back, the whole experience only sharpened the people skills I already had. If you can consistently convert someone from "fuck off" to "sign me up," the typical human interaction won't faze you much.

When it came to soft skills and communication, I surpassed most, if not all, of the more educated people in the program. It didn't matter how smart you were because if you weren't good on the phone, you never got the chance to demonstrate your knowledge. If you couldn't spark interest within the first 20 seconds of the conversation, you were done – game over, nice try, better luck next time.

See, I learnt to play to my strengths and address any weaknesses along the way. Technical knowledge, I could learn on the job, but street smarts were the result of a lifelong education not everyone gets. They don't teach everything in schools, and I believe that certain skills, such as effective communication, are crucial for success. The skills I learnt on the streets definitely helped me in my earlier days.

THAT'S A FACT

Being able to effectively articulate your ideas is a powerful skill. It's one thing to be super smart but if you struggle with communication, you'll have a hard time utilising others to help you reach your goals. No matter what business or career you're in, effective communication drives performance.[15]

With that in mind, it's no surprise that highly skilled communicators have the potential to make the most money, as businesses value these skills above all others.[16] Of course, you'll need to back up those soft skills with hard skills and knowledge but if you want to thrive in business and in life, effective communication is key.

HONESTLY, THEY COULDN'T BELIEVE IT

It won't come as a surprise, but many of my family members and friends were shocked at how I managed to turn my life around. While working in the mines and playing the stock market wasn't so surprising, becoming a successful financial planner was well beyond what anyone could've imagined. There was definitely a time when *I* couldn't imagine it. Sometimes it still feels like a lucid daydream.

I think every step of my journey shocked quite a few people. First, I got a job in the mines. Then I held that job and worked my way up to foreman, which was basically a leading hand role. Next, I got myself an advanced diploma in financial planning. Suddenly, I was a paid intern at AMP. Before they knew it, I'd been poached by one of the fastest-growing practices in the country.

My success may seem sudden and shocking to people, but it was far from a rapid process. I spent years building myself up to a point where I was capable, competent, and could make these things happen. I realised early on that every goal I reached built up my confidence, along with my hunger for the next thing. *What else can I do?* With each success, I'd push a bit harder, and it started to become a game of life. I surprised myself with my ability and how powerful the mind can be when we have the right mindset and determination. Why limit yourself? Why hold yourself back? Why not aim as high as possible? The more I succeeded, the more I wanted to find out exactly what I was capable of.

For me, it was about defying the odds in life. Compared to many others, I didn't have the worst childhood, and I didn't come from the worst circumstances, but, as you know, I wasn't particularly privileged either. After all the self-doubt, doubt from others, people giving up on me, it felt good to turn it all around and shatter everyone's expectations. Most people thought I was destined to waste my life and never amount to anything. Don't get me wrong – I fully understand why they thought like that.

Hey, I thought it myself for a long time. The way my life was tracking, it looked like I was going nowhere. Nowhere good, anyway. Self-belief. Willingness to change. Deciding enough was enough. That was what it took to get me on a better path. I had a burning desire to do better and provide a better life and future for myself and, hopefully, one day, my family.

As I achieved new levels of success, confidence, and self-belief, I started to realise that unwavering determination was part of the secret recipe for success and achievement. I noticed many people around me who were just as clever or talented as me but weren't achieving in life, often placing limitations on themselves. So, I decided to keep pushing and building the life I wanted, not just for myself but also to show others that, with the right mindset, knowledge, and plan, success is achievable for anyone.

When we want to achieve big things in life, we must start with conscious thought. What do I mean? When Steve Jobs originally conceived the iPhone, for instance, nothing like it existed in the world. Apple's engineers must have thought he was batshit crazy when he told them what he wanted to do. Apps, music, touchscreen, camera – all this jam-packed into one small device. See, the iPhone didn't happen by chance. Steve Jobs knew what he wanted to create, and he pushed his team to make it happen. Without a doubt, he met resistance and doubters along the way, but it didn't stop him. He had a vision, and he saw it through to the end. Now we have multiple iterations of the iPhone and its many competitors to show for it.

"Don't let the noise of others' opinions
drown out your own inner voice."
– STEVE JOBS

While my accomplishments baffled some people, I wasn't the only success story to make it out of a tough environment. Several people who I grew up with also managed to pull themselves out of poverty and find ways to get ahead in life. Many of us now own businesses and are doing well for ourselves. Over the years, we've pushed each other to perform, forming a powerful support network. Your circle is important, remember? You want the people around you to enhance you, not hold you back.

I should also mention that I think Uncle Keith must have been one of the most shocked at my success. Years later, I almost bought a business where he was a client, but I *just* missed out on the opportunity, as an internal employee of the business decided to take it over. Can you imagine if the deal had gone through? Uncle Keith would've been a client of *my* business, and I would've been in charge of his financial planning. It would've been a nice cherry on top, but I think I'd proved myself enough by that point.

A CLASHING OF VALUES AND IDEAS

Russ and I disagreed about a lot. We were from different generations and had different values, which came out once we were in business together for a bit. He was very old-school, while I wanted to be on the cutting edge. Russ didn't have a website for the company – he wasn't interested. This was well into the 2000s (around 2012) mind you, after websites practically became mandatory for any competitive business.

While Russ was very good at what he did, he was less adept at keeping up with the times. He wasn't thinking ahead and wasn't embracing new technology as it became available. Don't get me wrong, the business was booming, but it could have done even better if it had evolved with the times. I wasn't thinking about the 'right now'. Instead, I was thinking about the business I'd acquire in the next 10–15 years when Russ completely retired. I needed the business to still be there and be just as successful when I was ready to take over.

When we bought the $2-million-dollar business and went into partnership, I became the face of that business. We structured it as a subsidiary company, using the same back-office team. When I began running the business, Russ still mentored me. He had the experience, and I still had a lot to learn. Also, even though I'd put a big chunk of my own money into the deal – I had to sell one of my properties and take out a big business loan just to finance my contribution, which was around half – he still owned half the business. Even though we were partners, he still felt he should have the final say in every decision. This was where the problems started.

Initially, we had a good couple of years, building the company up and making decent money. Anyone would think I was living the dream, and, on paper, I was. I was the corporate suit and tie guy, making over $300K a year, and, outside of Russ's family, I was first in line to buy him out of the business when he was ready to retire. If all went well, I'd be loaded before I was 45 and could retire or sit back and enjoy the benefits of all my hard work.

Don't fuck it up, I kept telling myself. *You could become a multi-millionaire, just don't fuck it up.*

If I followed Russ's formula and did exactly what he'd done, I knew I could make millions. It worked for him, and he'd taught me the entire process. So, why didn't I feel like I was achieving my dreams?

Sometimes, on a Friday, we'd stop work early to catch up over nibbles and drinks. One afternoon, we had this enormous platter – cheese, salami, olives, all the good stuff. Anyway, it was massive, and there was heaps left over after everyone had finished and was starting to head home for the weekend, so I decided I'd take the leftovers to the soup kitchen across the road. When I explained what I was doing, people looked at me like there was something wrong with me. Here I was, wearing a nice suit, earning $300K a year, running and partnering in a successful practice, and I wanted to give cheese to the homeless. To my colleagues, I seemed insane. None of them had grown up poor or around housing commission families, so they didn't understand the struggle people faced. To them, the poor and homeless didn't exist.

"What, why would you do that? Just throw it in the bin."

It never even crossed their minds that the leftover food could feed someone who actually needed it. These were successful people. Where was their compassion? They were just like the people I'd seen at the train station all those years ago, pushing their way past a struggling, old lady. That was them, but it wasn't me.

Reflecting now, people don't know what they don't know, but, when this occurred, I felt like I was the only one who could see others struggling. Looking back, I believe this was the beginning of my own self-reflection, perhaps fuelled by guilt related to the life I was living.

In my career, I'd kicked all the goals – wealth, success, and, with several decades still ahead of me, a lot more room for growth – but I didn't feel fulfilled. I wanted to innovate within the business and take it down a different path. Why not help the underdog? I wanted to help the mum and dad who were struggling. I wanted to help the young person who hoped to get ahead but didn't have a spare 10, 20, 50 grand surplus lying around each year for the financial planning fees, let alone to invest. That's what some of the bigger practices charged their high-net-wealth clients – up to $50K a year. For many, the help they needed was financially out of reach. Finally, however, I had the skills and knowledge to really help people, and I wanted to take the business in a more meaningful direction.

Of course, more meaningful often means less profitable, and Russ would never let it happen. To him, I was just an overeager kid with too many ideas and not enough sense. My job was to shut up, know my place, and keep doing things by the book. Russ's book, that is. In his book, there was no room for innovation and definitely no room for contribution by helping the less fortunate improve their lives and futures. There was, however, plenty of room for anyone who was already doing well financially. But what about someone like me before I turned my life around? What about all the single mums out there, just like mine? What about all the housing commission kids, starting at zero when they enter the adult world due to the circumstances they were born into? Where was the contribution? Where was the innovation?

If I was a good boy and just listened and played by Russ's rules, I might have been in a position to buy the entire company in ten years' time. But if we didn't innovate, the company wouldn't be here in ten years' time. I truly believed that. I thought for sure the business would implode, but I underestimated Russ's financial capacity, which allowed him to survive hits that would've destroyed a smaller company. If he didn't have money to burn, who knows where the company would've ended up? It's amazing what you can do and survive when money isn't an issue.

I'd spent the past two years in business being money-driven, doing it Russ's way, and I'd achieved my vision for myself, but the soup kitchen incident made me question the path I was on. Did I really want this multimillion-dollar future? Did I really want to follow in Russ's footsteps? Did I want to be like him? We were two very different people, and he'd made a lot of money, while I wanted to help the underdog, who, let's be honest, isn't going to bring in a lot of revenue. Some of the most ruthless, and wealthiest, businesspeople don't care about collateral damage when it comes to making money. It doesn't matter who gets hurt, as long as profits are good. Just look at all the major corporations around the world. Those CEOs would sell their own mothers to raise the share prices of the companies they're running. That wasn't a mentality that aligned with my values. It wasn't a mentality I could adopt. It just wasn't me.

After that realisation at the end of Friday afternoon nibbles, I started to see things for what they were. I started to remember why I went down the path I did, who I was, and what my values were. Yes, I still wanted to make millions of dollars and be successful, but I believed it could be done in other ways. If I had to be exactly like Russ to get there, I'd give it all up in a heartbeat. I wouldn't sell my soul to the devil and become the same type of person I once despised. I'm not saying people from good families, who had good upbringings or are simply successful in life, are evil, but many lose themselves along the way, and I wasn't raised like that.

I was having an identity crisis of sorts, torn between two worlds, two versions of myself. There was the new, successful Kane, who wore a blue suit and a red tie and was making his mark on the corporate world. Then there was the deeper, authentic me, who was left wondering if he'd taken a wrong turn somewhere along the way.

Deep down, I wanted to build something meaningful, something I was passionate about, something *great*. I knew money was an important tool, but it couldn't be my sole focus. There's more to business – there's more to life – than that. But Russ didn't see it that way.

I did make some progress when we brought in a general manager, who created some genuine cultural change within the company. We began to focus on treating people well and reducing staff turnover, which, in my mind, was a solid step in the right direction. I tried to implement additional change, but I kept getting voted down and told I was being silly. The honeymoon period was well and truly over, and the whole miserable

experience was eating me up inside. I needed to do something...
but what?

Over time, our relationship grew more and more hostile, and
the situation turned ugly. Russ deactivated my security cards
and made me redundant from a company I was the director of.
Ruthless, right? Even as a director and 49 percent shareholder
in the company, I was booted out of the office and told I wasn't
allowed back. My wages were cut off, which, as a shareholder,
I obviously didn't agree to. When determining the distribution
of profits, all shareholders must agree on the decision, but Russ
completely cut me out.

After almost 18 months of legal disputes, which cost me over
$200K, we started to work out a solution that suited us both.
Well, it didn't exactly suit me, but Russ never worried about
anyone but himself. The deal favoured him, and he loved every
minute of making life hard for me during the process of sorting
it out. From this experience, I learnt one of my most valuable
lessons: business isn't personal, and some people don't play nice.
It opened my eyes to the legal system, shareholder agreements,
and company structures. There's a lesson in everything you experience. Some are just harsher than others.

When I started with Russ, there were around ten people in
the company. At the time of my involuntary exit, there were
22. For many years, I worked like a dog, listened to everything
Russ said, and hammered away at the business. I worked 10–12
hours every single day, which was a habit I started when I first
entered the bank as an intern. With Russ's mentality, this practice continued without question. As a sign of his success, he had
a 1.5-tonne aquarium installed in the office. It was glass either

side so as people exited the lift, they could see through into the entire office. What an entrance! It was like something out of a James Bond movie. The office was awesome. Russ did work hard to build it up over time, but my blood, sweat, and tears also went into that place, and I was practically forced out the door. Ultimately, however, it was for the best. If things hadn't turned sour with Russ, I might not have found a better path.

A TOXIC MENTOR BUT A MENTOR, NONETHELESS

Working for Russ, I didn't just get the opportunity to learn from him but from his entire team: the compliance manager, the investment committee, the paraplanning team – everyone had something to teach me. Each day, I had access to specialists, many with decades of experience, who I could extract information from.

If you want to learn something and don't have the time to self-teach, getting close to someone who already has that knowledge or skill set is a great move. Whatever you want to learn, chances are, someone out there can teach you. It's just a matter of finding that person and persuading them to share their knowledge. You could do this by offering your time or services in return for mentoring. Otherwise, access to experts and their knowledge could cost you money, but it may be worth it if you have no other options. Why not take the shortest route to your goals? Learn from the experts. Importantly, be intentional about what you want to learn. Why waste time learning something you'll never use? My high school self asked this question many times... The point is, if you're smart about it and utilise the people around you, you can fast-track your journey to success. If you don't have the right people around you, it's time to change that. Surround yourself with people who can help push you towards your goals.

During my time with Russ, he walked me through the acquisition process three separate times. For the inexperienced, it's a daunting and complex process, and I saved myself a lot of time and effort by having a seasoned pro like Russ as a mentor. He may have been a ruthless man, but I can't deny that I learnt a lot from him. Russ was the stepping stone I needed to get to the next stage of my journey.

Later, I realised that while he had the skills, knowledge, and experience I wanted in a mentor, our core values and visions didn't align. We were both pulling in different directions. If I'd realised this sooner, I would have sought a different mentor, but I ultimately learnt a valuable lesson, which I'm passing on to you now.

BIGGEST INSIGHTS FROM THE FIFTH CHAPTER OF MY LIFE

Focus on your strengths – Especially in the beginning, if you don't have a lot of knowledge and skill, you need to play your strong hand to get started and gain momentum. You should also address any weaknesses and try to improve upon them, especially if they're relevant to your goals. To succeed in my field, I needed to fix my grammar and verbal vocabulary. As I worked on improving these skills, I fell back on my strengths to keep me moving forward in my career. Some weaknesses won't even be relevant to your goals. Don't get too caught up on those. Everyone has weaknesses, and we can't fix them all. We can, however, let our strongest attributes shine through and address those that fall short when necessary.

Creative thinking – Thinking outside of the box is a great habit to develop. In the school system, we're conditioned to believe that every question has one answer and those answers – to pass an exam, for example – can only come from one source, such as the assigned textbook. But that's not how the real world works. The real world has been built by people who think outside of the box – often well beyond the box. I encourage you to develop a more creative, less constrained way of thinking to solve problems, overcome challenges, and achieve your goals. You might be surprised by what you can accomplish.

Play your own game – During my internship, when I began to do better than many of the other interns, some people in the program chose to focus more on me than themselves. They weren't trying to mirror what I was doing, which, in my eyes, would've been the smarter approach. Instead, they chose to criticise me and try to take me down. Essentially, they were looking for an excuse as to why I was ahead and they were falling behind. Don't do this in life. Don't compare yourself to others. It's a complete waste of your focus and energy. I quickly realised that I could make the most progress by focusing on me and my results and not looking back or to the side to see what others were doing.

My focus was strictly directed forward, towards my goals, my destination. Fuck what everyone else was doing. Social media will show you other people's visions of success, picture-perfect lives, and the best ways to make money. Don't be fooled. They're not your vision; they're not your life. Block it all out and focus on *your* vision, *your* goals, and *your* life. In the end, nothing else matters.

Self-belief – When you've put in the work, made the right sacrifices, and taken the time to learn and grow, opportunity will come knocking – but you must be ready to open the door and walk through it. You must be willing to accept what you've worked so hard to earn. With confidence built through meaningful action, consistent focus, and unwavering commitment to your goals, when those opportunities do appear, you'll be ready to take them with conviction, because you'll know you deserve them.

Stay true to yourself – While I believe in having mentors and coaches, I don't believe in letting them change you to become like them. In the pursuit of wealth, I almost let this happen to me. It can happen to anyone who's not careful and lacks a strong vision. I've seen success change so many people. Throughout your entire journey, it's important to remember who you are and who you want to become. I know so many people now in retirement who regret a lot of the things they did to earn their wealth and success.

Most of them didn't have a strong vision for their family, relationships, or personal growth. Their vision solely focused on money and career. Don't make the same mistake.

KANE WITH BEN SIMKIN

KANE WITH GRANT CARDONE

KANE WITH GARY VEE

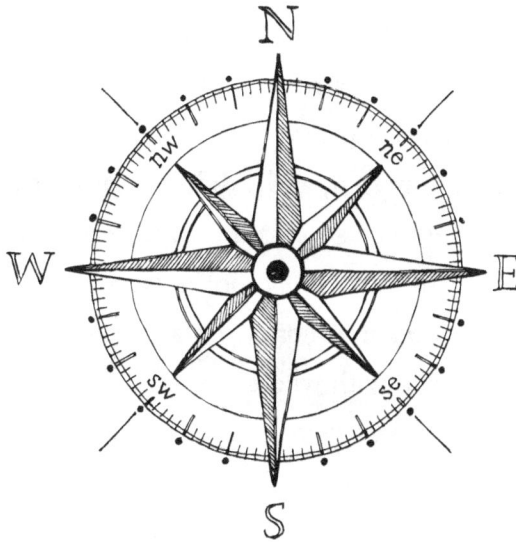

CHAPTER 6

CONSUMED BY WINNER'S GUILT

IT MIGHT SOUND WEIRD, BUT SUCCESS CAN SUCK

When I left Russ, I didn't know what to do next. I was lost. As many people do when they're looking for answers, I went down a bit of a spiritual path, getting into yoga, meditation, and Buddhism. For real. I was never a spiritual or religious guy, but I was trying to find myself, and I didn't want to leave any stone unturned. I wanted to be successful, make money, and be happy. Isn't that what we all want? The problem was, while I had become successful and made good money, I wasn't entirely happy. I felt empty and unsatisfied with where I was in life. The goal is to feel content, and I just wasn't there yet.

There's more to life than being successful in the traditional sense. As I found out, money isn't necessarily the best marker of success. Yes, monetary goals are important for most people, but the aim should be financial freedom to create a certain lifestyle rather than just chasing numbers. Most of us just want more free time to do the things we enjoy with the people we care about. The trick is figuring out how to make it happen.

While I was deciding what to do next, I spent a lot of time travelling, exploring Europe, China, and other parts of Asia, spending quite a bit of time in Bali. My family on my dad's side came from a place called Lofoten in Northern Norway, so I visited their hometown and spent time travelling through Scandinavia.

Clearly, I was on a bit of a soul-searching journey. *What do I want to do with the rest of my life? Who am I?* I knew I wasn't Russ, but I didn't know *who* I really was. I didn't even know if I wanted to focus on finance anymore. I started to wonder if I'd taken the wrong path. It didn't feel right anymore. If success meant becoming one of those corporate robots who're blind to reality, the reality I saw growing up, I didn't want it. *But,* I wondered, *does it have to be that way?*

As I went through the process of selling my share in the business – that is, Russ offering me a shitty buyout deal and me taking it – I started to think about what we really do as financial advisers. Importantly, I thought about what I *wanted* to do. The more I thought about it, the more I realised finance was only a part of the picture. What we did wasn't finance-related, not really. It was *lifestyle*-related. Why did people want to improve their finances? Because they wanted to live a certain lifestyle, no matter where on the wealth spectrum they fell.

At the time, my brother was living in a van in Byron Bay, making ends meet with the bare minimum and, importantly, loving life. I, on the other hand, was constantly stressed, even though I had more money than I thought I'd ever make. I had achieved financial freedom. So, why didn't I feel free? My brother was happy living in a van with barely a dollar to his name. Where had I fucked up? I'd chosen a certain path, and I'd sacrificed a lot to walk it, but it hadn't brought me the fulfillment I thought it would. What was I missing? Here I was, with enough savings to take a year off to travel the world, while some people were struggling to scrape enough together for their next meal. Wherever I went, my values always travelled with me, driving my thoughts and actions. Had I done enough to help others like me? Had I done enough to help those who'd not yet broken the chains of trauma, poverty, and neglect? The system was failing them, as it had failed me, but I'd found a way out. I realised I hadn't really turned back to help others find the right path and escape the system. That was the problem. I'd crawled out of the shit to get to where I was, but I hadn't stopped to show anyone else the way out, the way to a better life. Instead, I'd used all the skills and knowledge I'd accumulated to help people who already had money make more money. But what about all the struggling kids? What about all the single parents who work hard and live honest lives? Don't they deserve to know all the tips and tricks for creating better lives for themselves and their families?

I thought back to what I'd witnessed in housing commission and how disadvantaged those kids were right from the start. It was almost as if they never had a chance to thrive in life. But they did have a chance, didn't they? As we know, I wasn't the most hard done by kid, but I didn't have it easy. I had to work hard to make the most of the shitty hand life had dealt me, and I'd seen others who'd had much tougher lives than me do the same. With the right mentality and support, anyone can pull themselves out of a seemingly hopeless situation. None of the people I knew growing up were beyond hope or beyond help, whether they believed it or not.

Suddenly, I knew what I had to do.

COMING FULL CIRCLE

Finally, I understood that success isn't just about business and money. It's also about who you are and how you treat people. What are you contributing to the world? There's more to life than accumulating resources. Yes, money is an important tool, but, as I learnt, it'll leave you feeling hollow if you aren't living out your values and creating the impact you want.

I knew I wanted to help people turn their lives around, but I didn't know how. I was still trying to find the path forward when I found the answer in a local newspaper. Or, more accurately, Mum put the answer right in front of me.

"Do you remember Michelle, the PCYC police youth officer?" she asked, thrusting a newspaper in front of me.

How could I forget? "Yeah, I remember Michelle," I said, taking the paper. "What about her?"

"She's on the front page."

No shit... That was definitely Michelle, right there on the front page of the paper, being acknowledged for all the awesome things she'd done, all the amazing programs she'd created to help troubled kids, programs like the one I'd once been a part of. Sometimes when you've got a question, life puts the answer right in front of you. You just have to be paying enough attention to recognise it.

Now, Michelle and I hadn't talked in over ten years, so imagine her surprise when I got in touch and explained the trajectory my life had taken. She was blown away, astonished that I wasn't in jail and had instead pursued a successful career in finance. To her, I was the success story she and her programs needed. Basically, they needed a poster boy (or girl) to promote the benefits of their juvenile programs, as they relied heavily on government funding. If they couldn't show clear results, the programs could get canned. Finally, I'd found a way to give back.

Instantly, I jumped in and got involved in the PCYC, running fitness programs on Wednesday mornings and mentoring kids in the Big Brother program. I even fostered a kid full-time. His name was Dylan, and he was 16 years old. But here's the crazy thing: I later realised that I'd known him when he was 2 years old. When I was living in housing commission, Dylan lived next door, so I understood a bit of what he'd experienced growing up.

I spun out when I realised who he was. It was as if my life had come full circle. I was back where I started; I'd returned home, but I was a completely different person, with knowledge, wisdom, and experience to share. I felt like I was closer than ever to finding my true north.

GIVING BACK – THE CURE FOR WINNER'S GUILT

As I established this new version of me, I started giving talks and got referred to different PCYCs around Australia. I also started speaking at high schools, sharing my story and advice with young people doing it tough. I even went back to Boys' Town, where I gave talks and got involved in creating their marketing videos. Eventually, I became the first former Boys' Town student to join the board, ending up as a foundational board member, helping develop change for the facility and the programs they were running.

Over the years, the PCYC and Boys' Town (Dunlea Centre) programs have evolved so much, and I can't explain how amazing it is to see and be a part of the change. Who would've guessed I'd end up back at Boys' Town in that capacity? Not me, that's for sure. Not my friends. Not my family. Not anyone who knew me when I was a juvenile delinquent, smoking in the streets and telling the police to piss off. I don't blame people for being blown away when they see what I've achieved – but it didn't happen overnight. It took over ten years for me to come full circle. As you know, I spent that time working on myself, applying myself, pushing myself to change. Change doesn't come easily, but, with commitment and discipline, it's absolutely possible to achieve.

The experience of talking to kids, engaging them in conversation, offering whatever insights I could was an honour that was 100 times more rewarding than any amount of money I'd earned or any deal I'd made in business. The fulfillment I felt far surpassed anything I'd experienced as a successful adviser, earning six figures a year.

I now understood that money alone can't make us happy. We need a purpose beyond simply lining our pockets, generating wealth if we want to feel fulfilled. Before, I'd had it all wrong, but now I understood I could have it all. Thankfully, I wouldn't need to live in a van, like my brother, to be happy. I could have happiness, fulfillment, *and* financial freedom if I could figure out how to make this new direction work.

When I gave talks, some places tried to pay me, but they never offered much. Frankly, they couldn't afford much. I was talking in public schools with shoestring budgets. Sure, I could've spoken at private schools, where there was more money to throw around, but my story wasn't relatable to those kids. They weren't the ones who needed to hear it. The talking, the mentoring, the giving back – it wasn't how I wanted to make money. My goal was to give, not take. Even if I could've made it work financially, it wouldn't have felt right, limiting support to only those who could afford it. That's the problem, right? The privileged get everything they need, while the disadvantaged have to fight for it every step of the way.

To me, money was still important. If I wanted to make the impact I imagined, I needed financial freedom and a good amount of wealth behind me. At the same time, money *wasn't* important. I knew it couldn't be my primary focus; otherwise, I'd end up lost, resentful, and full of winner's guilt again.

Plenty of kids were standing at the same crossroad I'd once found myself at. *Do I resign to a life of crime? Or can I achieve something more, a better life?* It could be as innocent as coming from an underprivileged household, feeling stuck, and lacking self-belief. At one time, that was me, and, as we know, I could've easily taken the wrong path, as so many do.

A plan, a vision started to form in my mind, and I could see a future where I generate wealth *and* give back at the same time, helping those who need it. Financial freedom, or service to others – I didn't have to pick just one. Truth be told, I could have both. I could build a business that was profitable while still contributing positively to society.

The foundation for True North Lifestyle was laid.

THAT'S A FACT

Contributing, giving back, and having a purpose can improve your mental health.[17] When we have purpose and focus on helping people, we improve our own lives while also improving the lives of others. Pretty good deal, right?

If you're feeling lost, down, and perhaps a little purposeless, remember, the science says that giving back is a great way to boost your sense of happiness and fulfilment.[18]

CREATING A (TRUE NORTH) LIFESTYLE

Why True North Lifestyle? Why not True North Financial or something of that nature? Like I said, as a financial adviser, most of what I did for clients was lifestyle- not finance-related. While helping clients kick financial goals, I was also helping them craft the lifestyles they desired. When I built True North, I wanted exactly what we were doing to be clear. It's not about the money – that's just a tool to get you where you want to go. It's about the lifestyle you want to achieve. It's also about knowing the rules and how to play the game to get there easier.

I wanted my services to be accessible to as many people as possible. Of course, I still had to make money and keep the lights on, but any revenue I generated would simply be a tool to keep taking my vision to the next level.

I knew what I was doing; I knew the system, and I knew how to make money work for people instead of the other way around. With True North, the primary focus would be measurable goals around lifestyle, which we'd achieve through financial strategies. Finally, I had the opportunity to innovate in ways I couldn't when I was working with Russ.

Of course, I took a big risk by building a business that wasn't primarily profit-driven. It's a bit of a counter-capitalistic approach, yeah? When you're in business, making money is supposed to be the aim, or so we're led to believe, but not everyone thinks that way. The thing is, if you play the game right, you can create a company that makes money *and* aligns with your values. You don't need to build a business with a profit-at-all-costs mentality. At least, that's what I wanted to believe.

STRUGGLE AND SACRIFICE, WE MEET AGAIN

In the first six months or so, True North limped along, barely making enough to cover the overheads. The crappy buyout deal from Russ meant I didn't have a lot of money to pour into the business. Then there was the royal commission into Australian financial services, which couldn't have come at a worse time. Government changes to one legislation meant that, at the stroke of a pen, my business lost over $500,000 in equity – that is, value – and experienced a 25 percent drop in total revenue. If I'd stayed with Russ, the change wouldn't have put more than a dint in the business, but it almost crippled True North. The reality was, external factors were at play, and it was out of my control.

When times got tough, I couldn't help but question whether I was on the right path. I certainly wasn't pulling in the $300K salary I'd made with Russ. By choosing the direction I chose for the business, I'd put its viability at risk. Was I wrong? Should profit always be the main goal? Should everything else come second? Was it the only way to survive in a cutthroat corporate world? *Fuck no.* I wouldn't accept it.

Even though the business was struggling. I wasn't broke – far from it. I still had some money in the bank and assets I could sell to keep the dream alive. I'd chosen my path, and I'd stay committed to it. To me, giving up wasn't an option, so I sold a house I had in rural New South Wales and used the money to pump up the company capital. With the new capital, I bought another business using the acquisition strategy Russ had taught me. It was a small business, owned by a retiring adviser, but it was in decent shape. Over time, I cut back staff, pulled way too many 10–12-hour days, and built the company up, living off a lean $25K a year. The sacrifices were necessary and worthwhile because when our financials were strong again, I bought another business, bigger than the first, and we experienced 350 percent growth in less than two years. From there, we were able to fund marketing and begin to build the staff back up.

If I'd gone into True North with the mindset that I'd be killing it immediately, making a six-figure salary and buying oversized fish tanks for the office, I would've been very disappointed, and I likely would've failed. Instead, I was prepared to eat shit for a couple of years and work myself to the bone because I knew that was the pathway to success. Thankfully, I was right. Man, I don't know where I'd be now if I'd got it wrong. Luckily, I didn't need to find out.

THE KEY TO BECOMING A SKILLED ANYTHING

"A smooth sea never made a skilled sailor."
– FRANKLIN D ROOSEVELT

My mate Kris is an entrepreneur who'd had a pretty rough upbringing. He had a tough life early on, but he pulled himself out of his shitty situation and created a better life for himself. When I was building True North Lifestyle, working long hours and fighting to turn a profit, I could turn to Kris for advice and support. He knew what it was like to struggle and what was required to be successful when you were coming from behind. He also understood the strength we gain from overcoming adversity.

Talking with him one day, I came to a realisation. Firstly, I wanted to be an entrepreneur, not simply a business owner. I wanted to innovate, push the boundaries, and create a positive impact in the world. Now, I already knew and was trying to achieve these things, but, until then, I'd never made the *conscious* decision to pursue entrepreneurship and do what it took to earn my stripes in the business world. Previously, I'd had Russ supporting me through every step of my business journey. Looking back, I'd always had the entrepreneurial spirit, but I never quite knew where to channel it, especially when I was younger. Now, I had an outlet *and* the freedom to explore this path, without anyone holding me back.

Secondly, I realised that to be a successful, experienced entrepreneur, I needed to face adversity. I couldn't just stroll into success and have everything go my way from the get-go. Building True North was a struggle, but it was a struggle I needed to undergo. You can't gain real experience or truly test yourself when building a business in good times. To become a master of whatever it is you want to do, you must face adversity and overcome it. I'm not saying you should try to make things difficult for yourself, but every challenge is an opportunity for growth, and every opportunity should be welcomed.

From a business perspective, after starting True North, I was practically bankrupt within six months, struggling to claw back revenue lost after the royal commission. On top of that, I no longer had the backing of Russ and a multimillion-dollar practice to smooth the rough seas ahead. Essentially, I was on my own. Thankfully, I still had personal assets, which I did use to fund the new business, but, in a way, I was starting from scratch. More accurately, I had over $1 million dollars in debt hanging over my head, so I was technically starting from behind. At the time, the whole thing seemed a little unfair, considering what I'd built and achieved in the few years prior, but I quickly realised it was exactly where I needed to come from when creating True North. It had to be a struggle, a true passion, a labour of love. We haven't truly tested ourselves until we've faced and overcome adversity. Without struggle, we can't truly know ourselves or our potential. I felt that I had to walk through the fire, and prove I could survive it, before I could call myself an entrepreneur – so that's what I did.

Through the whole process, I could see the light in the distance, and, eventually, we made it out of the dark. Once True North Lifestyle was on the path to becoming everything I imagined it would be, I was finally free to start focusing on my other goal and passion: supporting the disadvantaged.

Because I took another hard road to success, I was stronger and more resilient than I would've been otherwise. When COVID hit, do you think I was rattled? I didn't even flinch. In fact, we boomed throughout the pandemic because I was quick to adapt and careful not to react. Times were tough for a lot of businesses, but I'd dealt with tougher times, and the stress and uncertainty didn't faze me so much. I'd learnt from the challenges of the past.

That's how you become a skilled entrepreneur, a skilled *anything*. You have to sail the rough seas because that's where you'll learn your biggest lessons.

THAT'S A FACT

Often, our mindsets around the adversity we face can be more detrimental than the adversity itself. When dealing with struggle and difficult challenges, the mindset GPS can help you navigate them more easily.[19]

So, what's the mindset GPS? I'm glad you asked!

- **G**rowth – A growth mindset understands that people can improve and skills can develop through learning and a willingness to try.
- **P**urpose – Having a clear purpose helps us push through the hard times, as we know exactly what we're fighting for and why.
- **S**ocial – Strong social connections are the foundations of our lives, but they don't happen overnight. They take time and effort, which is something we must remember if we ever feel deficient in this area.

On your journey to success, let your GPS be your guide, and you'll be much more likely to arrive at your destination.

IF I'M GOING TO LEAVE, I MIGHT AS WELL LEAVE A LEGACY

Through True North Lifestyle, I've helped countless people turn their finances around and create the lives they want – on their terms. The problem was, I could only impact so many people at any given time working one on one. Also, as much as I wanted to help everyone who needed it, I still had to turn a profit. Unfortunately, I couldn't work for free. But that didn't mean I couldn't find a way to help more people in a scalable and cost-effective way. I was an entrepreneur now, and innovation was always going to be a big part of my business.

Plenty of people need financial advice but aren't ready to invest in financial planning. I had to accept the fact that the full advice service we offer at True North Lifestyle wasn't suitable for everyone I wanted to help. I needed to find a middle ground, something tailored to the people who were ready to take control of their finances but didn't know where to start. How could I share my knowledge and help people create their ideal lives in another way?

With my goal of helping more people in mind, I created an innovation plan for the business. One part of my plan was this book, a simple and inexpensive way for people to learn from my experiences and expertise. I doubt I'd be where I am today without all the books I read in the mines as I tried to crack the code to success. The next big innovation was True North Academy, a platform for providing education through online courses and access to money coaches and a like-minded community – and it has been an absolute game changer.

Through online courses and coaching, I'm teaching people how to take control of their finances and, therefore, take control of their lives. The more you understand about society's systems, tricks, traps, and the rules to the game of life, the better you'll be able to use them to achieve your goals. We often fear what we don't understand, and with knowledge comes a sense of power and control.

But I'm not stopping there – not a chance. There's a reason why I'm still pulling 10–12-hour days, slaving away in my own business when I don't really need to anymore. If I didn't have a pretty ambitious aim for the future, I'd hire a few extra staff, sit back, and enjoy a much shorter work week – but I'm not built like that. For better or worse, I can't just sit back and take it easy because, frankly, I've got big goals and dreams beyond creating a life for myself...

See, we know that money is a useful tool, and, for what I plan to build, I'm going to need a truckload of it. Before I leave this planet – and I mean in the traditional sense, I'm not going to Mars or anything like that – I want to contribute much more than I already have. I want to leave a *legacy*. So, when the time is right and my finances are where they need to be, I want to step away from the day-to-day operation of my businesses and start a charity, with the aim to buy a big rural property somewhere, a farm. Why would I do something like that? Because I want to build a retreat where disadvantaged youths can receive the guidance and mentorship they need. I want to create a charity that makes a genuinely positive impact in the world and in the lives of the people who need it.

When I finally create it, I don't want to be 65 years old and not have the time or energy to enjoy it. I want to be fairly young and have the charity up and running before my kids grow up so they can be involved in what will be a major contribution to the world.

I imagine a self-sustaining farm, with fruits, veggies, free-roaming chickens, rescued horses and dogs, all of that, where kids can learn real skills, develop as human beings in a positive way, and see the world through new eyes, not focusing on the pain, the struggle, and the suffering. It's a lofty goal, right? As you've probably noticed, I'm not short of ambition or drive, and if it can be done, I'll make it happen. The question isn't if but *when*.

One day, I'll achieve my goal, and I'll be on a farm somewhere, helping troubled kids turn their lives around. And when I'm gone, the farm will still be there, helping people well into the future. That's what I want to give to the world. That's what I want to create. That's the legacy I want to leave.

Don't get me wrong, I also want to have great businesses that contribute to the world and help as many people as possible find their true north. I want my kids to have a good upbringing and have everything I didn't. I still want a flexible work-life balance, several holidays a year, a nice house, and money to help my family when needed. Right now, I take over 12 weeks off each year, regularly travel overseas, and live a couple hundred metres from the beach. If my immediate family needs help, I'm in a position to provide it. I've already achieved these big, important goals, and I've realised I can do more. How far can I go? What else can I achieve? What more can I give to the world? That's where the charity and all the other work I do to help the less-fortunate, the kids from lower-income households, who haven't had a good start in life, comes in. By the time they turn 18, they're already well behind the start line – but I want to change that. Everyone should have the opportunity to do well in life.

THE RIGHT PATH

To me, it's important to be there in the trenches with these kids. I can't understand them or what they're going through if I'm sitting in an office somewhere, disconnected from the people I'm trying to help. I was on the board at Boys' Town for three years, and I did what I could to help the organisation. The programs are amazing, and the organisation is now accredited to do the year 10 school certificates. It's also on its way to being able to provide the HSC to kids wanting to further their studies.

However, being a board member wasn't the right fit for me because I wasn't on the front line where I felt I could have the most impact. I wanted to be directly involved in the programs, working with kids, interacting with them, having those life-changing conversations. Often, when I gave talks in schools, the naughtiest kids would approach me afterwards and open up to me, sometimes breaking down in tears. Maybe Dad was in jail or Mum was battling cancer. They always had a pretty fair reason for acting out. They just needed someone to give them the time of day and actually listen to what they had to say, which was exactly what I needed when I was labelled the naughty kid at school. When someone feels safe and comfortable enough to open up to me like that, it's an honour and a privilege. None of my achievements, not even my success or wealth, compare to having one of those kids open up to me. They don't even come close. It's overwhelming, euphoric even, to share those life-changing moments with all those young humans.

When I help someone find hope or self-belief, it's the most rewarding feeling in the world. I never knew how powerful helping and guiding others could be for myself and for them. What we offer to the world could be the thing that changes someone's life forever, just like Michelle, Gerard, and even Beau and Danny changed mine. My journey is full of life-changing moments, and yours can be too.

I want people to know they have unlimited potential. I didn't realise it growing up but with each achievement, I better understood what I was, and anyone is, capable of.

Whatever you choose to do in life, it's important to stay true to your values. It's important to find your true north. I took a wrong turn when I pursued wealth along the cutthroat corporate path, but my values steered me back on track. When you're driven by values and passion, the energy you feel can't be explained. You have a drive that can't be stopped. If you're not feeling that drive in what you're doing, ask yourself, *Does it align with my values and what I'm passionate about?* If not, it may be time to correct course and get yourself back on track.

When you're on the right path, you'll know it. You'll *feel* it, and nothing or no one can stand in your way.

You have one life on this planet, and your time is limited, so spend it with those you love or doing what you love. Before you know it, you could be stuck in a relationship, job, or circumstances you hate, unable to find a way out. It's time to change, break the cycle. Do it for you and your future self or family. From this point forward, you have the power to choose your path. In fact, you always had that power. Don't get me wrong, it will require some work, perhaps a lot of work, but if you're true to yourself and your heart, the effort will be more than worth it because you'll be living life on your terms. So, get out there and find your true north!

If you want to learn exactly how to play the game of money, cultivate a mindset for success, and take control of your finances, I'd love for you to join me at True North Academy (www.truenorthacademy.com.au). Or if you'd like direct help managing your finances and creating financial freedom, our doors are always open at True North Lifestyle (www.truenorthlifestyle.com.au). I hope to see you soon!

KANE TALKING TO KIDS AT YOUNG LEADERS EVENT

KANE TALKING TO YEAR 12 STUDENTS

KANE WITH GENERAL MANAGER AND STAFF AT BOYS' TOWN

BIGGEST INSIGHTS FROM THE SIXTH CHAPTER OF MY LIFE

Clear vision and goals – One of the biggest insights I gained in my journey was that it's crucial to have a clear vision for all areas of life, and, of course, some accompanying goals. I've had mentors and clients who didn't understand this, or did too late, and they're now burdened with regret around the areas in their lives where they feel like they failed. So, from the very start of your journey, it's important to have a holistic vision and related goals that align with your values and your why. If I'd realised this sooner, I could've made better decisions early on and saved myself a lot of hurt and stress. In hindsight, however, I've always been someone who needs to learn the hard way. Hopefully, the same isn't true for you.

You deserve a break – Taking a break every now and then isn't failing or neglecting your dreams. Some will say you need to hustle 24/7 – that's bullshit. Make time for yourself and the people you care about and aim to create a balanced lifestyle. In the early years of my business journey, I drifted into burnout territory a few times, always chasing the next goal, especially when I had some momentum and felt like

I had to capitalise while things were going well. To be effective in the long term, you need your health intact. So, find whatever helps create balance in your life, whether it be yoga, meditation, the gym, running, fasting, day naps, juice detoxes – whatever helps you maintain your physical and mental health. Because you'll need to be at your best to chase those dreams down.

Struggle leads to growth – Adversity is a part of the journey of life. The moment I realised that adversities are opportunities to learn and grow, navigating them got much easier. It's all about handling your mindset and your emotions, while still making practical decisions. It's not always easy, but the adversities you overcome will help you reach the next level of the game. So, be ready for all those future adversities that come your way, because they're simply opportunities in disguise.

Give back – Find a way to give back. You can either start to do this early in your journey or later in life. When I found something more important than the typical services I was providing as a financial adviser, I got a second wind, a second why. Suddenly, I had a new goal beyond simply creating a better life for myself. I would also create better lives for others.

Michelle Dury came back into my life for a reason, and I recognised the opportunity for what it was – a chance to give back. So, keep your eyes open for those opportunities because they can lead to your greatest and most impactful achievements. Helping troubled, at-risk youths has been the most fulfilling work I've done in my life to date, providing a sense of fulfilment and purpose I can't explain. So, ask yourself, *What else can I contribute to this world before I leave?*

Find your true north – Finding and following my true north, being the most authentic version of myself in the pursuit of my vision led me to found True North Lifestyle, the business I envisioned. I'd finally realised one of my biggest dreams. Finding your true north is something only you can do. You decide your direction in life; you decide the terms by which you live it.

Personally, I found my true north when I realised money wasn't the end game. Having a purpose was much more important, and giving back became my end goal. As I followed my true north, True North Lifestyle and True North Academy were born. Through this brand and my businesses, I aim to give back and eventually create a charity that will serve a purpose close to my heart. Wherever you are in life, I encourage you to find *your* true north.

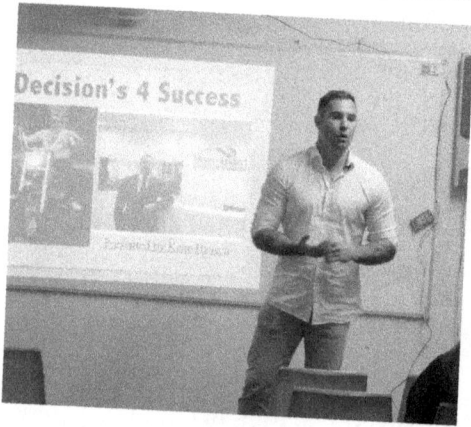

KANE TALKING TO
YEAR 12 STUDENTS

KANE TALKING AT HIGH SCHOOL

ACKNOWLEDGEMENTS

To the following people in my life who helped shape me and shared in some of the moments and memories that formed this book. I want to thank you all, along with everyone else who helped bring this book to life, allowing me to share my knowledge and story with the world.

To Michelle Dury, who had a massive impact on my life with the programs she ran and developed at the PCYC for many years. I believe these programs played a big part in changing my life. At the very least, they ignited my love for the gym, boxing, and maintaining a healthy lifestyle. Without the great work you do, many families and children would've missed out on hope, help, and opportunities that changed their lives. They would've become just another statistic, what we've come to accept as collateral damage to underprivileged and lower-demographic households.

To Gerard McDonell, who was a key influence around my thinking as a young teenager. When you or I thought my walls couldn't be broken down, even though you might have felt that you never got through to me or other kids, the work you did made a huge difference and helped me make the right decisions later in life. The values and standards you instilled into the boys at Boys' Town were something I never forgot, and I value your work and guidance during my time there.

To Dwayne 'The Rock' Johnson, who I've never met in person, though I feel like you had a huge impact on my world. From a young age, when trying to find who I wanted and needed to be to change my life and break the cycle of generational poverty and unrealised dreams, you showed me that anything is possible. With a good heart and a willingness to give back to the world, we can rise above our circumstances in life.

To those who I haven't listed or dedicated this book to but who were a big part of my life and the stories herein, those who shaped this book and me during my journey from struggle to success, you know who you are. Some of you are still in my life, and some are not, which is fine. You all had an impact on my life and helped me along the way, shaping me into who I am today and showing me that I can create a better life through hard work and a willingness to change. I still hold you and those memories close to my heart and have an unlimited amount of respect for each and every one of you. This book wouldn't exist without the real-life events and people in my life, both positive and negative, over the years.

ABOUT THE
AUTHOR

Kane Hansen is a financial adviser, business owner, entre-preneur, author, and a big proponent of giving back. As the founding adviser of True North Lifestyle, he helps people from all walks of life take control of their finances and build their dream lives. But his path to success has been far from smooth.

Following a series of devastating family events, including his parents' divorce and mother's cancer diagnosis, Kane's confused emotional state led him to be labelled a 'problem child', and he was expelled from the public school system. After expulsion, he continued his education at Boys' Town (now Dunlea Centre) in Sydney, a secondary school for at-risk youths. There, he learnt important life skills, practised discipline and routine, and formed some of his most critical values. In adulthood, he returned to Dunlea Centre in a much different capacity, running programs and joining the board as a foundational board member – a first for an ex-student.

Growing up in a low-income household with a single mother and multiple siblings, Kane entered the adult world at a financial and educational handicap. When a series of unfulfilling jobs failed to satisfy his entrepreneurial spirit, he began searching for an alternative path to success, eventually finding his way to the underworld.

Quickly realising he didn't suit that life, he left Sydney to work in a bauxite mine in the Northern Territory, where he moonlighted as a stock trader, learning how to play the wealth game through self-education and hands-on experience. Seeking to understand how to better manage his own finances, he completed a diploma of financial planning, later leaving a high-paying job as a leading hand to pursue a career as a financial adviser.

After being accepted into the Financial Planning Career Changer internship program with a large bank, through hard work and determination, he became a top performer among the other better-educated interns. His efforts didn't go unnoticed, and he was quickly employed by a large, successful practice. After a multimillion-dollar acquisition and partnership arrangement, a misalignment of values saw Kane sell his share of the business to start his own practice, True North Lifestyle. Through True North, Kane is able to help more people create the lifestyles they desire, focusing on smart money management and creating financial freedom. He believes that everyone should have the opportunity to develop strong financial literacy.

To help more people master their finances, in 2023, Kane founded True North Academy, an education platform that teaches everyday people everything from basic budgeting to how to play the money game, and win.

Coming from a disadvantaged background, Kane understands the struggles many people face, and he takes every opportunity to give back to the community. As well as serving on the Dunlea Centre board, he has worked with PCYC Australia since 2015, working on youth group sports and education programs. Additionally, he has worked with Project Youth since 2017 and takes frequent opportunities to mentor disadvantaged teenagers, encouraging them to set goals and strengthen their financial literacy. He is also involved in the foster care system, offering his time and care to those in need.

Kane's ultimate goal is to one day build a retreat for disadvantaged youths, giving them a safe place to set clear goals, create strong values, and learn practical life skills, helping them turn their dreams into reality.

When he's not working in his businesses or giving back to the community, Kane is spending time with his family – fiancé Petra and daughter Zara. He often takes time from his busy schedule to travel overseas, experiencing the world and broadening his horizons. Kane is an advocate of continual learning and self-improvement, and he is always looking for ways to better himself both personally and professionally.

www.truenorthlifestyle.com.au

www.truenorthacademy.com.au

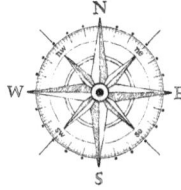

THE NEXT
STEP IN YOUR
JOURNEY

You know my story. You've learnt many lessons I had to learn the hard way. You know what it takes to create the life you desire – but you can always learn more.

We've designed a range of products and services to help you take your knowledge and life to the next level. For reading my book, you'll receive a $100 AUD voucher to use on anything we offer. It's my way of saying thanks for reading!

Go to **www.kanehansen.com.au** to take the next step towards your dream life.

ENDNOTES

1   Landry, L 2019, 'Why Emotional Intelligence Is Important in Leadership', *Harvard Business School*, viewed 2 June 2023, https://online.hbs.edu/blog/post/emotional-intelligence-in-leadership.

2   Keuschnigg, M 2023, 'The Plateauing of Cognitive Ability among Top Earners', *European Sociological Review*, vol 39, no 5, pp 820-833, viewed 23 January 2024, doi.org/10.1093/esr/jcac076.

3   Urquijo, I, Extremera, N, & Azanza, G 2019, 'The Contribution of Emotional Intelligence to Career Success: Beyond Personality Traits', *International Journal of Environmental Research and Public Health*, vol 16, no 23, viewed 23 January 2024, doi.org/10.3390/ijerph16234809.

4   Harvard Health Publishing 2020, 'Exercising to Relax', viewed 24 November 2023, https://www.health.harvard.edu/staying-healthy/exercising-to-relax.

5   Gleeson, B 2020, '9 Powerful Ways to Cultivate Extreme Self-Discipline', *Forbes*, viewed 24 November 2023, https://www.forbes.com/sites/brentgleeson/2020/08/25/8-powerful-ways-to-cultivate-extreme-self-discipline.

6   Kahneman, D & Deaton A 2010, 'High Income Improves Evaluation of Life but Not Emotional Well-Being', *Psychological and Cognitive Sciences*, vol 107, no 38, pp 16489-16493, viewed 24 November 2023, doi.org/10.1073/pnas.101149210.

7   Singh, D 2022, 'Human Values: A Case Study of Undergraduate Students', *International Journal of Research and Analytical Reviews*, vol 9, no 1, viewed 22 January 2024, https://ijrar.org/papers/IJRAR1CIP010.pdf.

8   Taylor, B 2018, 'What Breaking the 4-Minute Mile Taught Us About the Limits of Conventional Thinking', *Harvard Business Review*, viewed 22 January 2024, https://hbr.org/2018/03/what-breaking-the-4-minute-mile-taught-us-about-the-limits-of-conventional-thinking.

9   Lally, P, Van Jaarsveld, CHM, Potts, HWW, & Wardle, J 2009, 'How Are Habits Formed: Modelling Habit Formation in the Real World', *European Journal of Social Psychology*, vol 40, pp 998-1009, viewed 24 November 2023, doi.org/10.1002/ejsp.674.

10 Gerber, S 2018, 'Why Your Inner Circle Should Stay Small, and How to Shrink It', *Harvard Business Review*,

viewed 22 January 2024, https://hbr.org/2018/03/
why-your-inner-circle-should-stay-small-and-how-to-shrink-it.

11 Harrington R 2016, 'Don't Believe the Myth about Monkeys and Bananas',
Business Insider, viewed 18 June 2023, https://www.businessinsider.com/
wild-monkeys-do-not-eat-bananas-2016-6.

12 Gates, B 1996, 'What I Learned from Warren Buffett', *Harvard
Business Review*, viewed 28 June 2023, https://hbr.org/1996/01/
what-i-learned-from-warren-buffett.

13 CNN n.d. *Richard Branson on the Risk of Starting a New Airline in
the 70s*, video, viewed 5 December 2023, https://edition.cnn.com/videos/
business/2022/11/30/richard-branson-virgin-group-billionaire-risk-taker-
entrepreneur-cnntm-cprog-vpx.cnn.

14 Kiyosaki, RT 2017, *Rich Dad Poor Dad: What the Rich Teach Their Kids
about Money That the Poor and Middle Class Do Not!*, Plata Publishing,
Scottsdale, Arizona.

15 Baldoni, J 2009, 'New Study: How Communication Drives Performance',
Harvard Business Review, viewed 23 January 2023, https://hbr.
org/2009/11/new-study-how-communication-dr.

16 Chartered Accountants Australia and New Zealand 2017, 'The
Future of Talent: Opportunities Unlimited', viewed 23 January
2024, https://www.charteredaccountantsanz.com/-/media/
e5056e8aac9243f098fe7ba030ce7c88.pdf.

17 Parker-Pope, P 2020, 'The Science of Helping Out', *The New York Times*,
viewed 23 January 2024, https://www.nytimes.com/2020/04/09/well/
mind/coronavirus-resilience-psychology-anxiety-stress-volunteering.html.

18 Ritvo, E 2014, 'The Neuroscience of Giving', *Psychology Today*, viewed 23
January 2024, https://www.psychologytoday.com/us/blog/vitality/201404/
the-neuroscience-giving.

19 Hulleman, C & Happel, L 2018, 'Help Students Navigate
Life's Transitions with a Mindset GPS', *Behavioral Scientist*,
viewed 23 January 2024, https://behavioralscientist.org/
help-students-navigate-lifes-transitions-with-a-mindset-gps/.